# CHIHULY

## IN THE GARDEN

ATLANTA BOTANICAL GARDEN

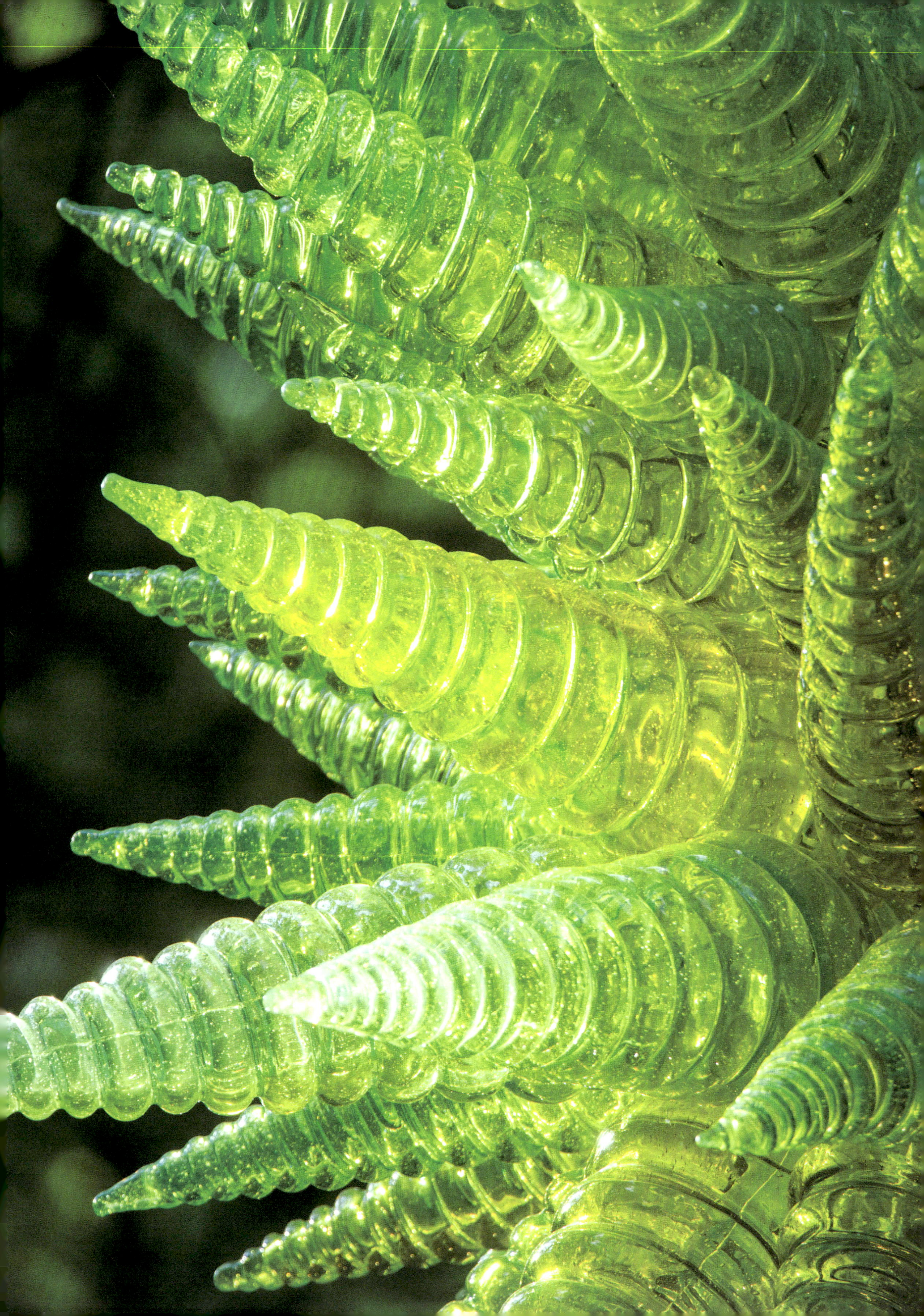

# CHIHULY

## IN THE GARDEN

ATLANTA BOTANICAL GARDEN

CHIHULY WORKSHOP

# CONTENTS

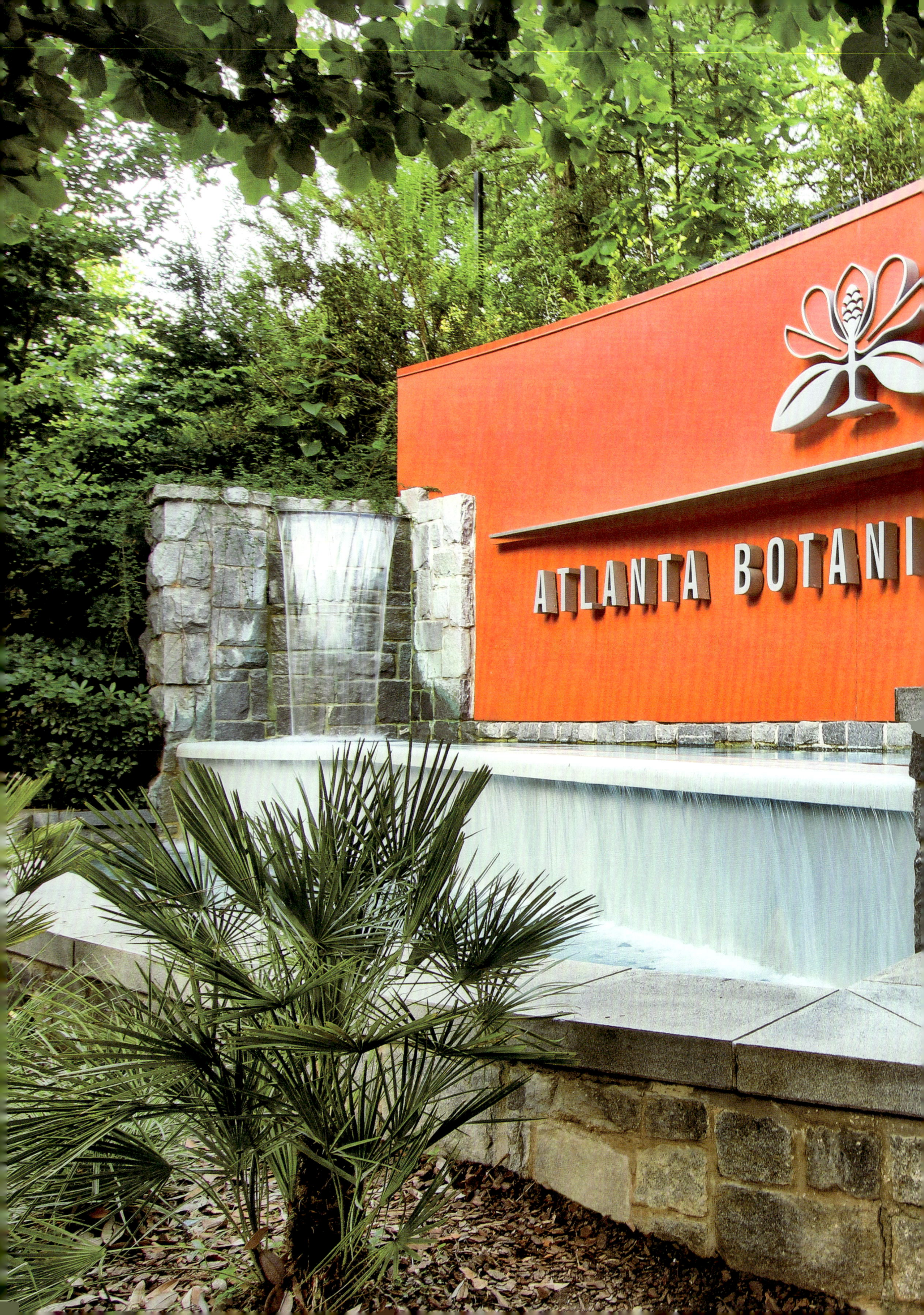
ATLANTA BOTANI

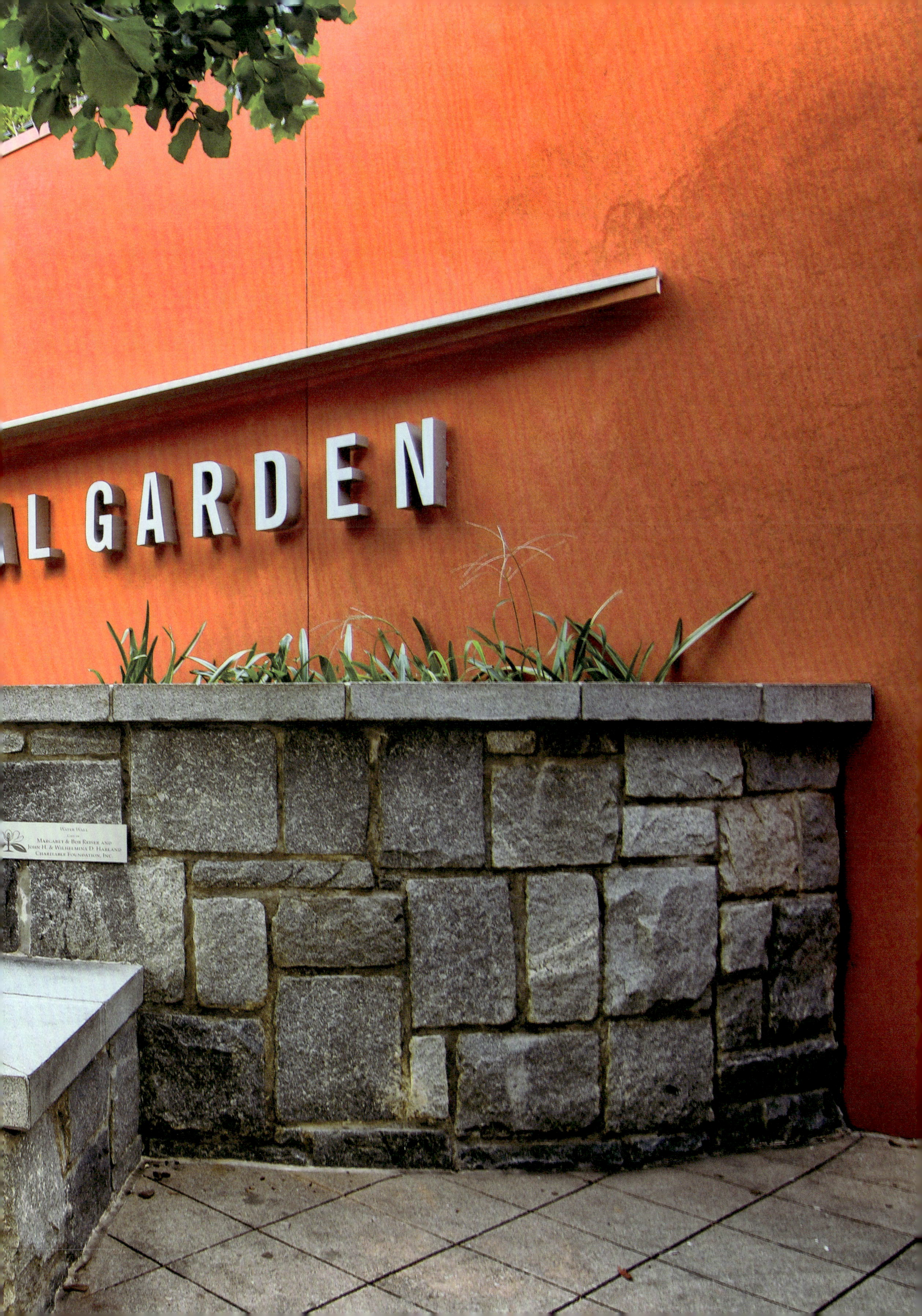
AL GARDEN
Water Wall
Margaret & Bob Reiser and
John H. & Wilhelmina D. Harland
Charitable Foundation, Inc.

# FOREWORD

Mary Pat Matheson
*The Anna and Hays Mershon President & CEO*
Atlanta Botanical Garden

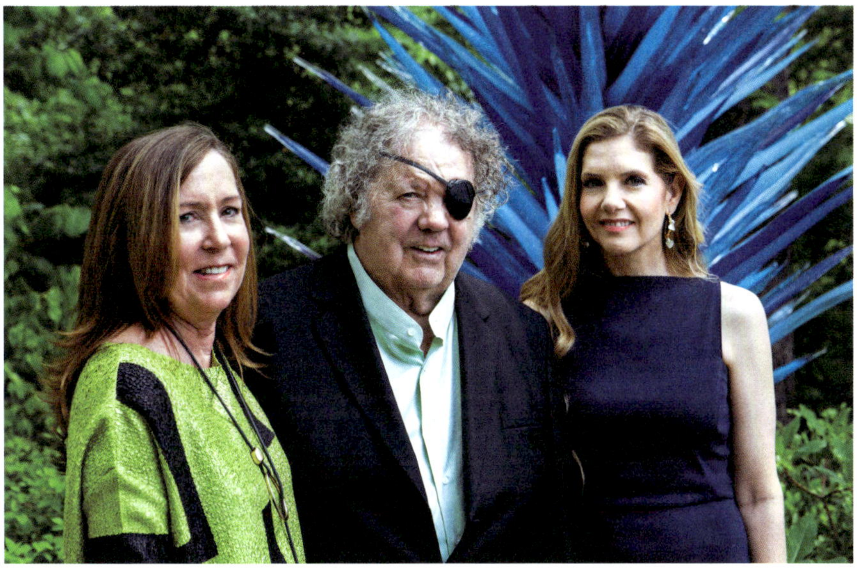

Mary Pat Matheson, Dale Chihuly, and Leslie Jackson Chihuly
Atlanta Botanical Garden, 2016

## Welcome to *Chihuly in the Garden*!

Thinking about Dale Chihuly and his magnificent art makes me both nostalgic about the past and excited to host another major exhibition of his wonderful works of art.

It's been twelve years since we first introduced Chihuly's work to the Atlanta community and the Southeast, and the Garden as well as the city have changed remarkably in that time. The 2004 exhibition was what I fondly call our "coming-out party," as it introduced the Garden to the greater metropolitan area in a huge way, doubling our visitation and membership. I loved seeing guests from throughout Georgia that year and was delighted to learn that more than 30 percent of our visitors were tourists.

Chihuly truly set the stage for the Garden's dynamic growth and success. The exhibition demonstrated that this beautiful garden was the perfect canvas for internationally acclaimed sculpture exhibitions, music, and much more. We also discovered the nighttime experience during the 2004 exhibition, lighting up the artwork and inviting visitors to enjoy *Chihuly Nights*.

Since the 2004 exhibition, I have never tired of the question that our visitors ask all the time: "When will Chihuly come back?" There is no other artistic expression that touches visitors like Dale Chihuly's art. The beauty is dazzling, forms compelling, and integration with plants beyond imagination.

And what better time to stage an encore exhibition of this magnificent artwork than 2016—the Garden's fortieth anniversary. This exhibition is remarkable on so many levels; the inclusion of neon in the woodland and orchid center adds a dimension that is beyond imagination. You will find several iconic works presented in new ways and three original installations created just for our Garden.

We are thrilled to welcome you as our guests, and we thank you for your support in our mission to connect people with plants. We are also extremely grateful for the support of our sponsors for this exhibition: The Home Depot, the Isdell Family Foundation, and the Forward Arts Foundation.

Cheers to Chihuly!

*Opposite and next*

**INDIGO BLUE ICICLE TOWER**

2015, 13½ x 7½ x 7'

installed 2016

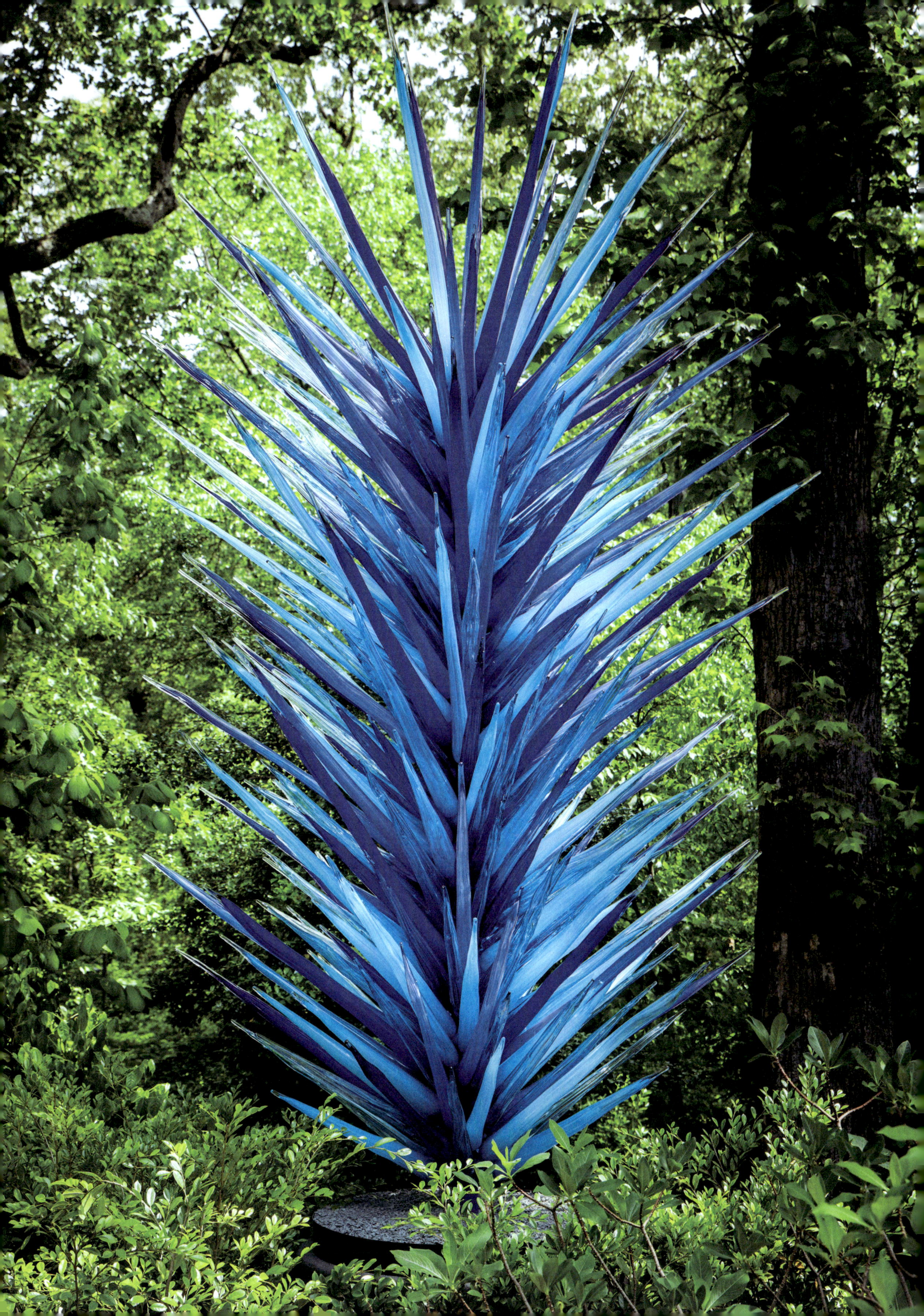

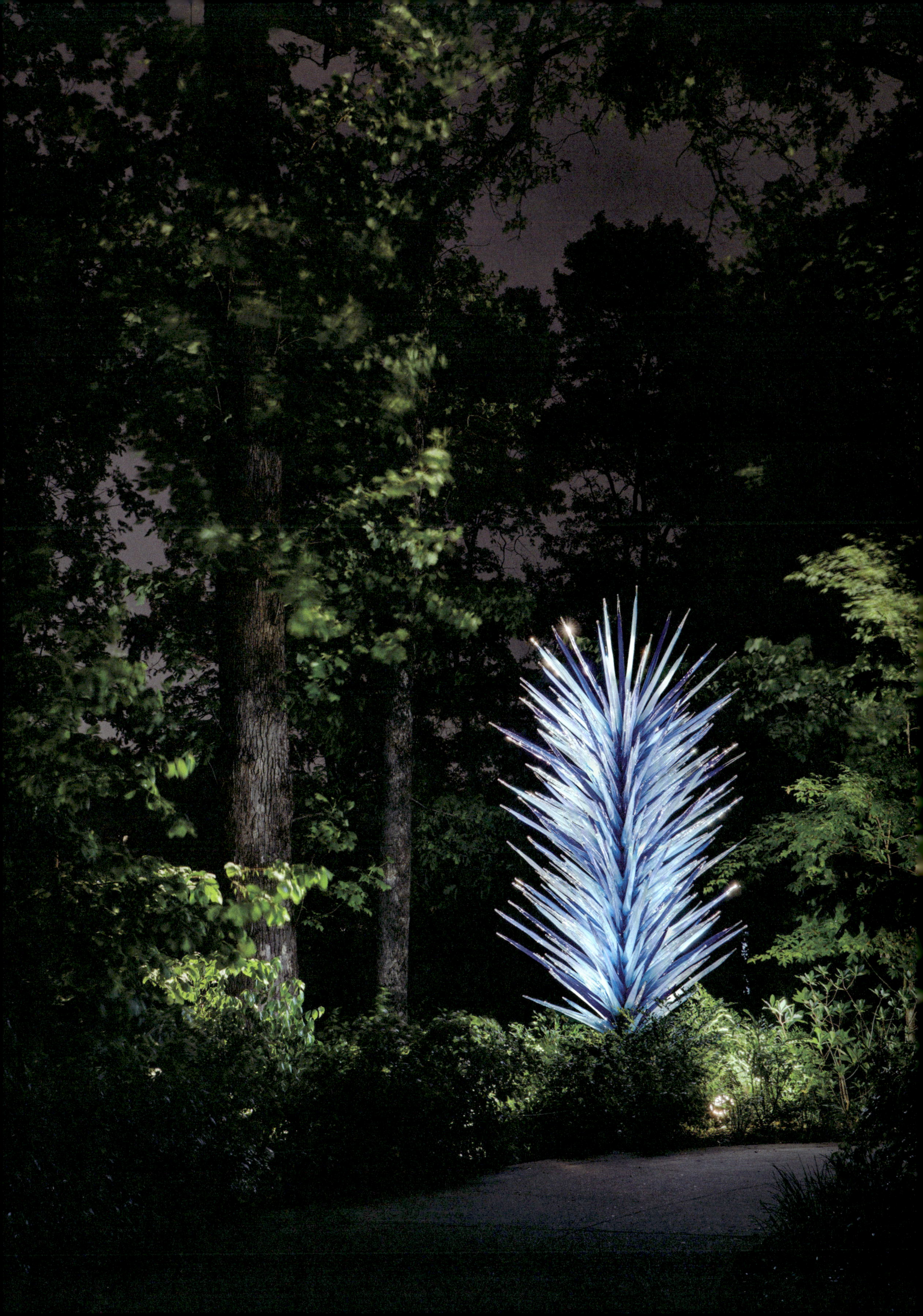

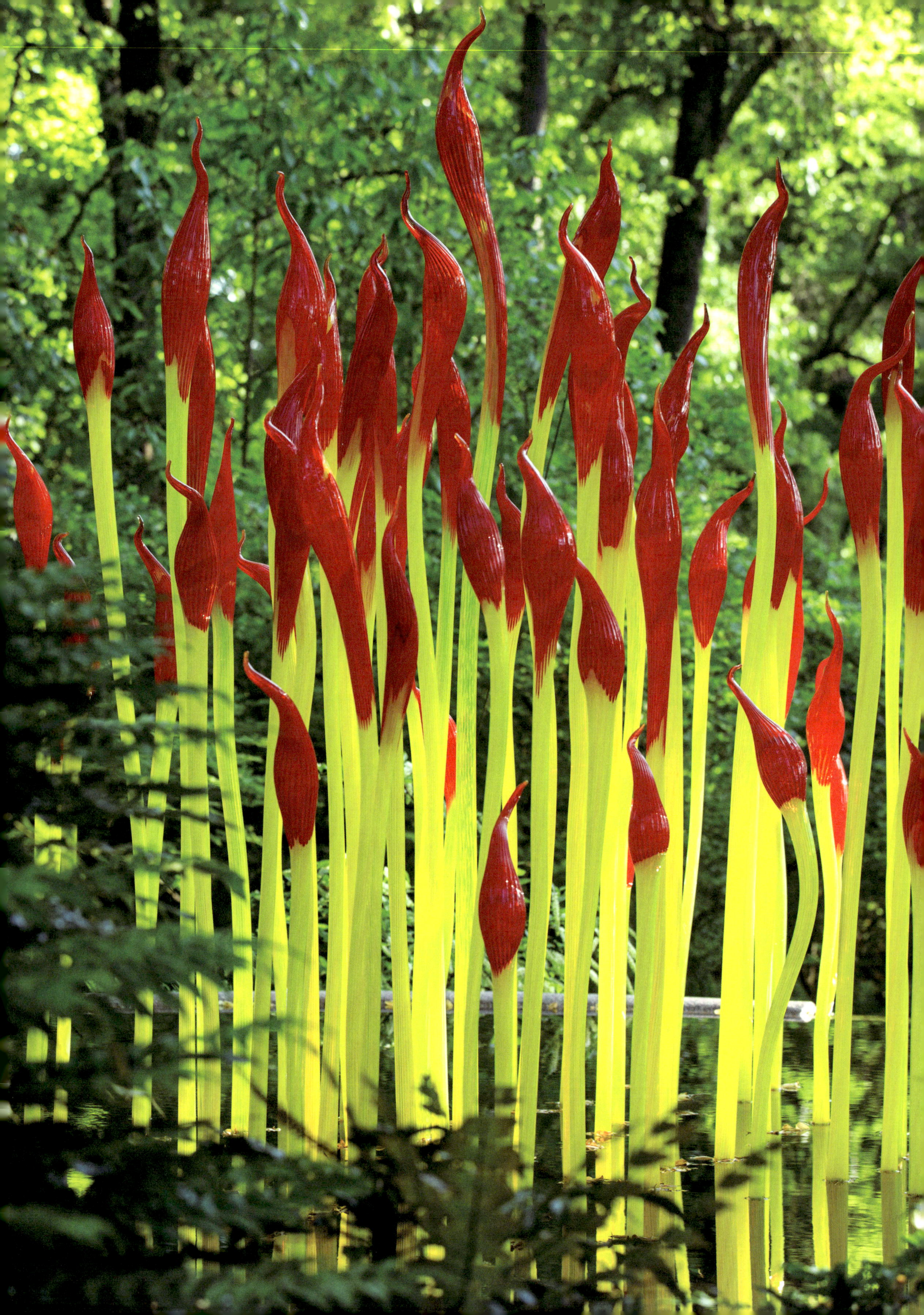

*Next (detail opposite)*
**FERN DELL PAINTBRUSHES**
2016, 90 x 88 x 76"

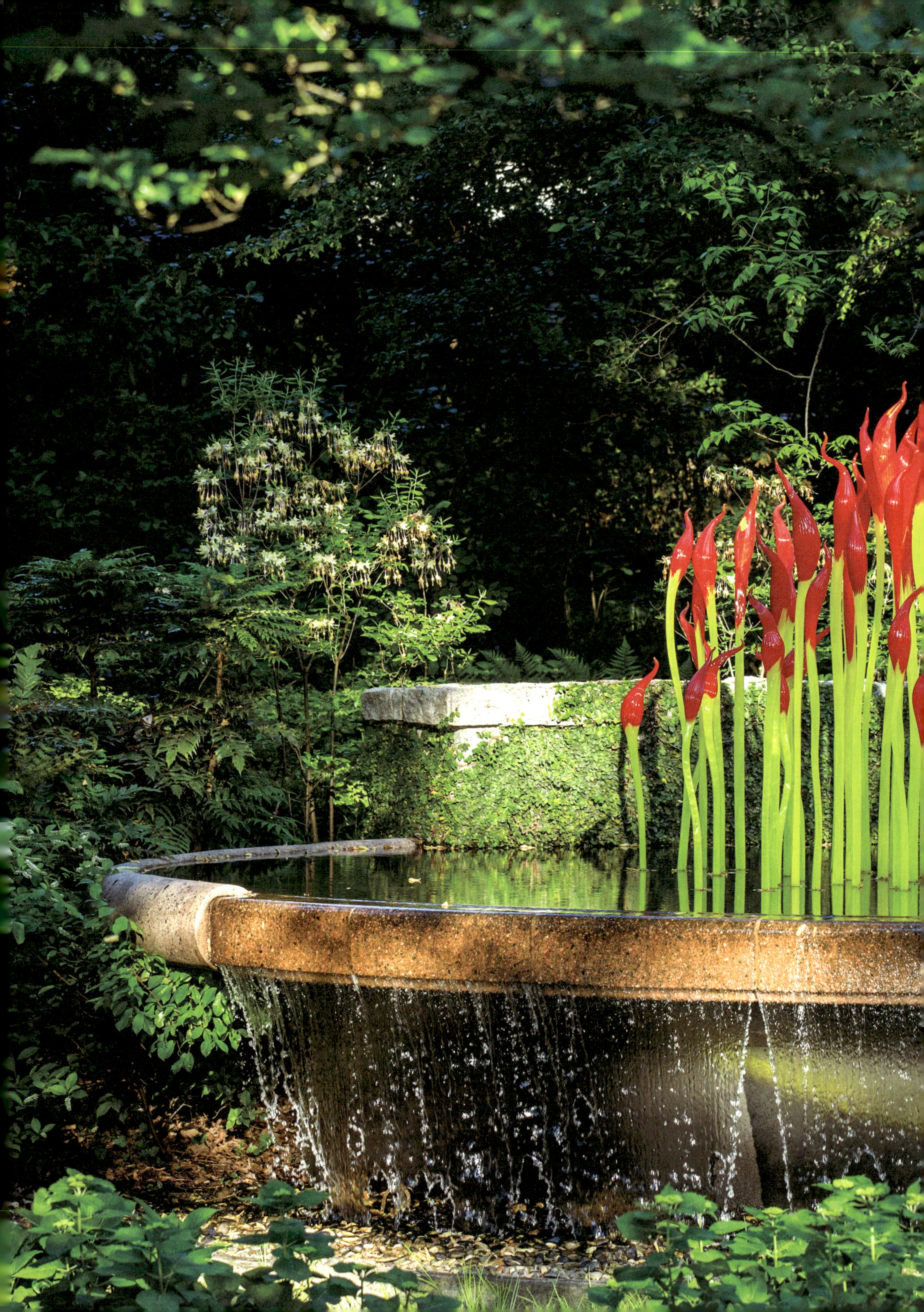

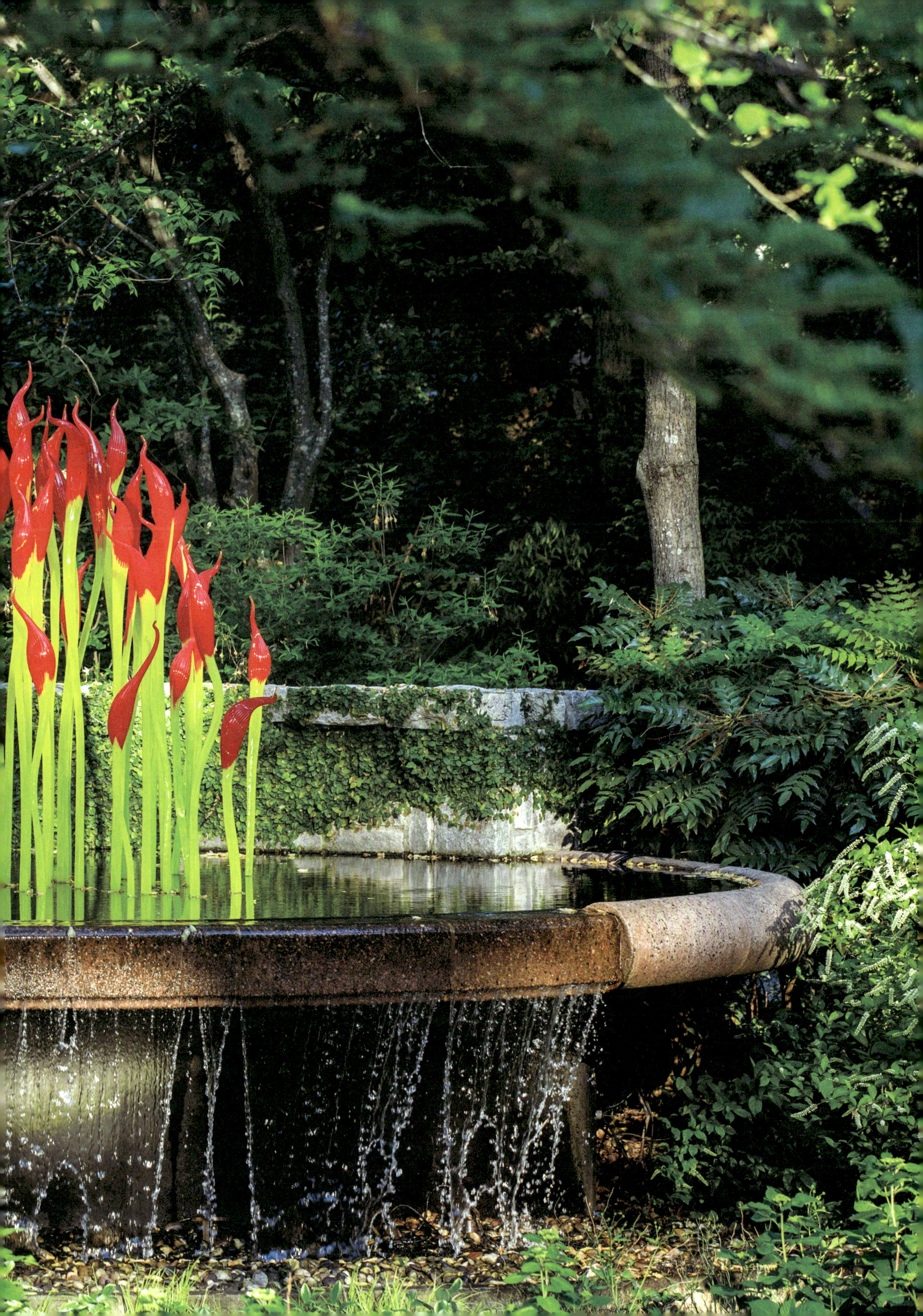

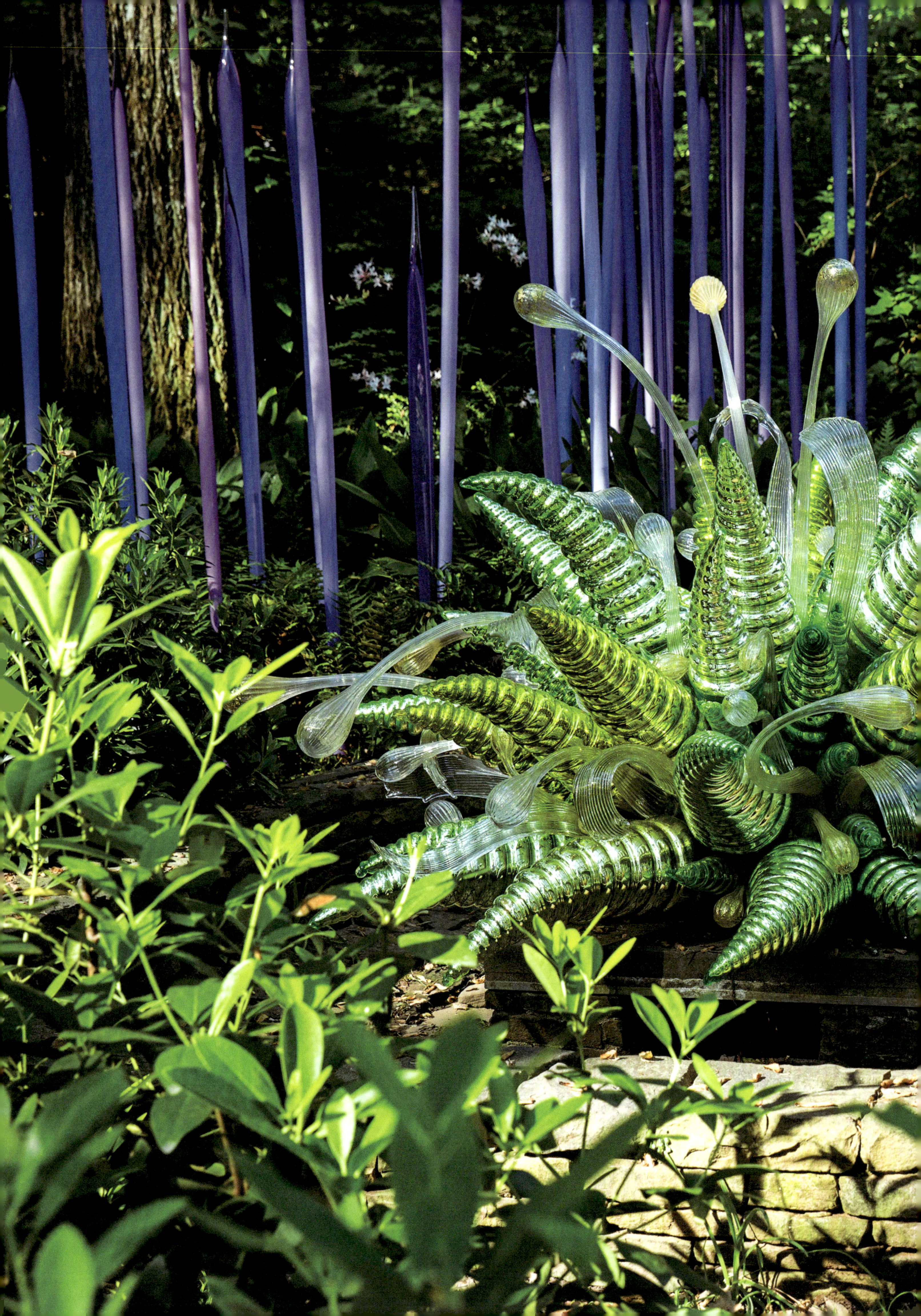

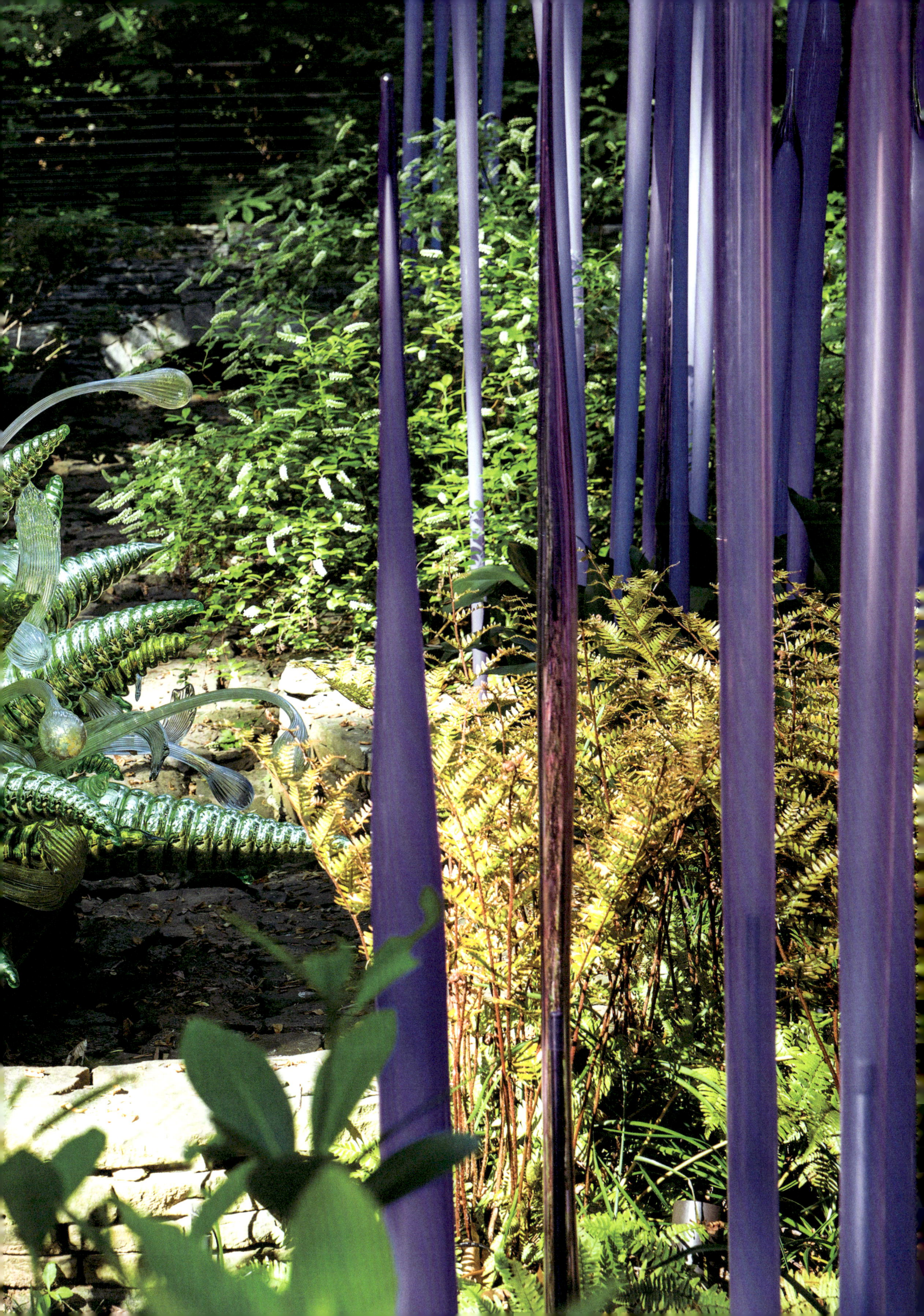

*Previous*
**NEODYMIUM REEDS**, 2014, and
**GREEN HORNETS AND WATERDROPS**, 2016
installed 2016

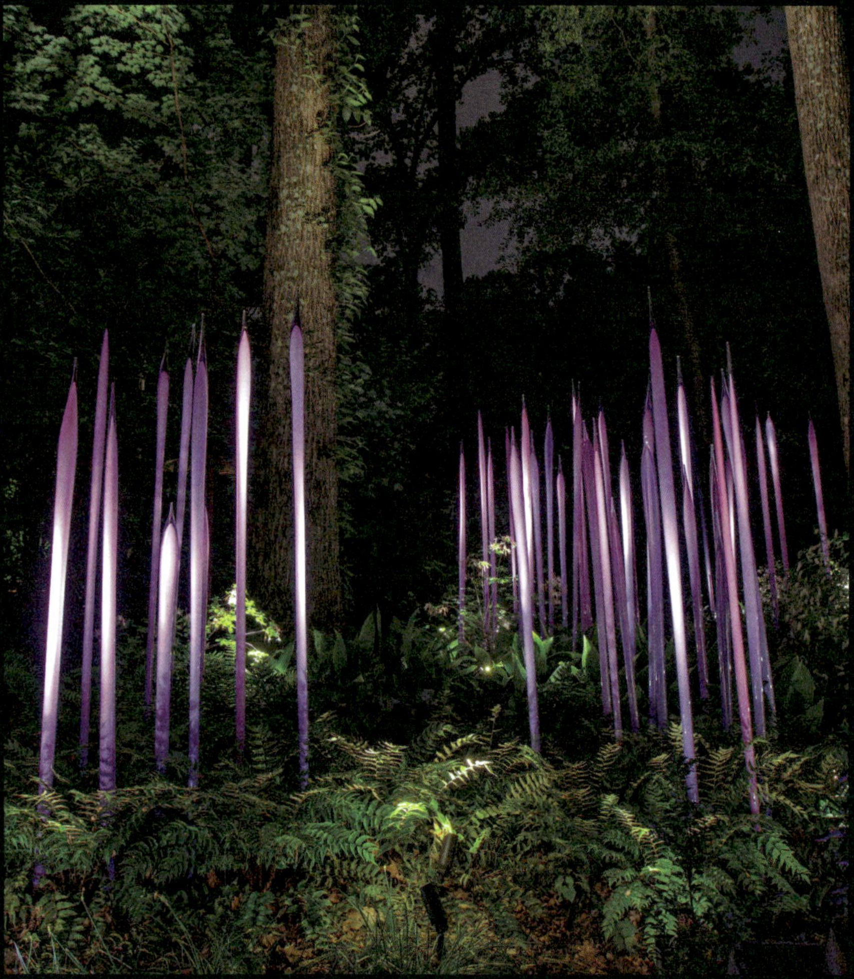

*Above*
**NEODYMIUM REEDS**
2014, installed 2016

*Opposite*
**NEODYMIUM REEDS**, 2014
**GREEN HORNETS AND WATERDROPS**, 2016, and
**CHARTREUSE HORNET POLYVITRO CHANDELIER**, 2001
installed 2016

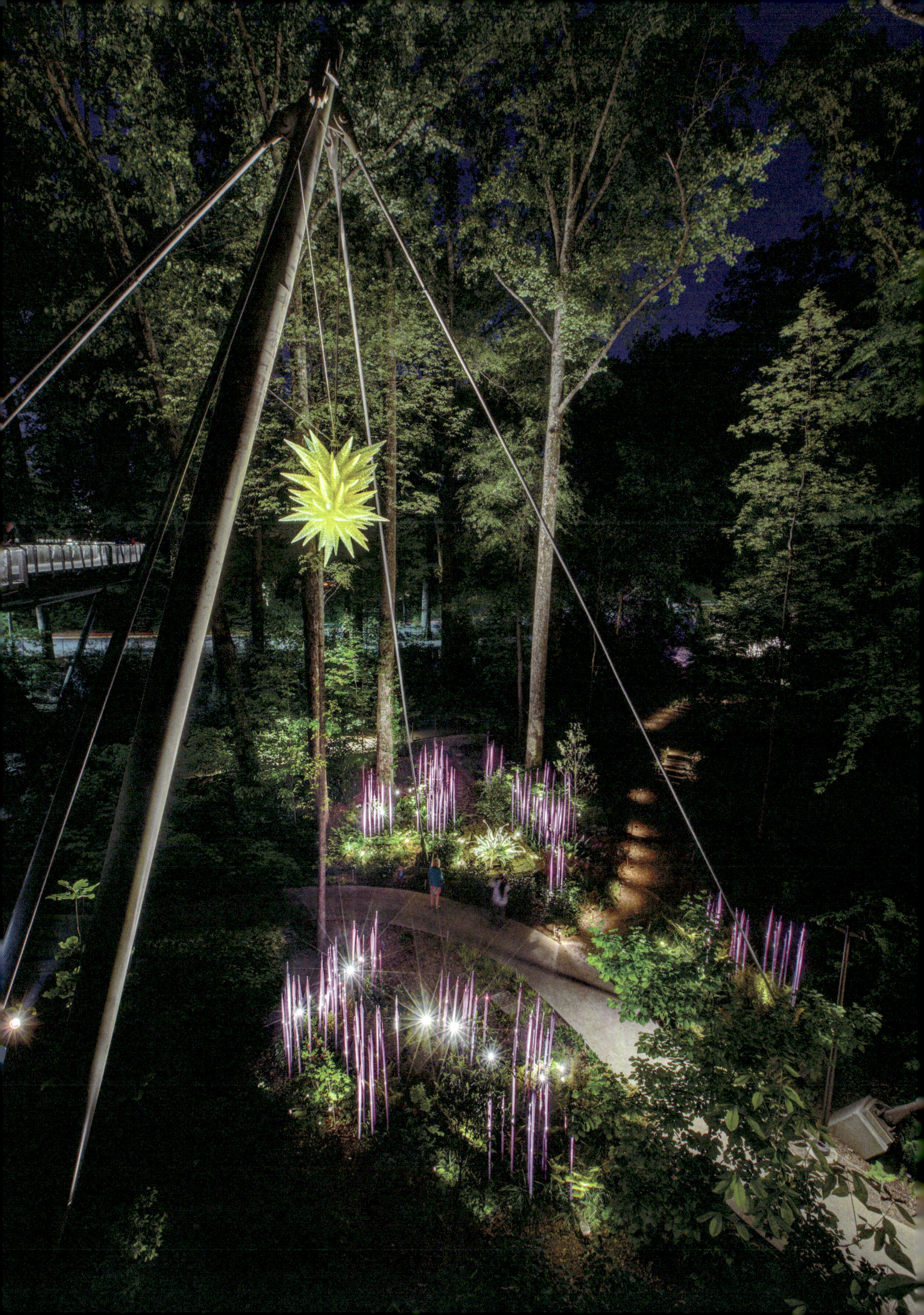

*Opposite*
**CHARTREUSE HORNET POLYVITRO CHANDELIER**
2001, 74 x 58 x 54"
installed 2016

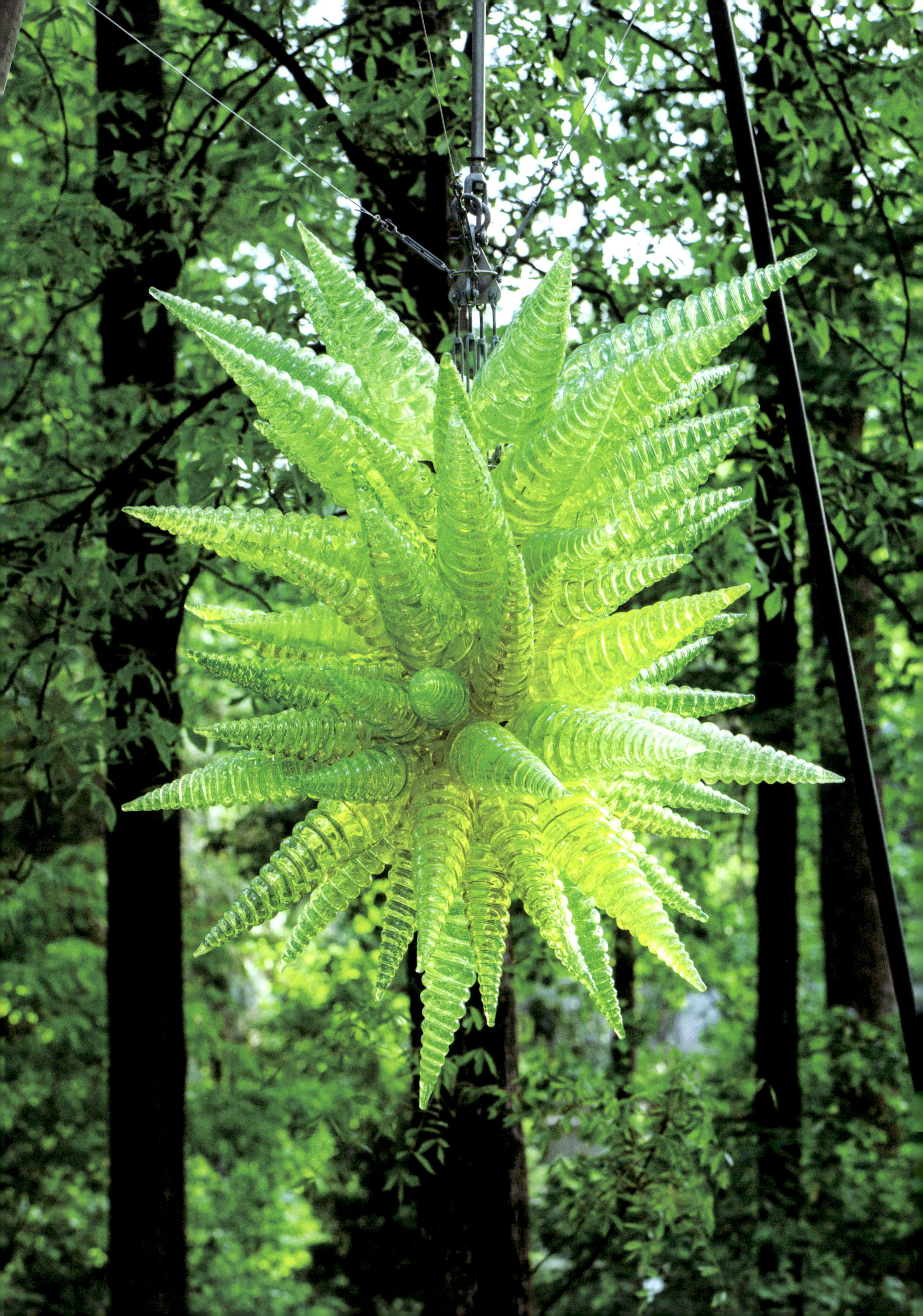

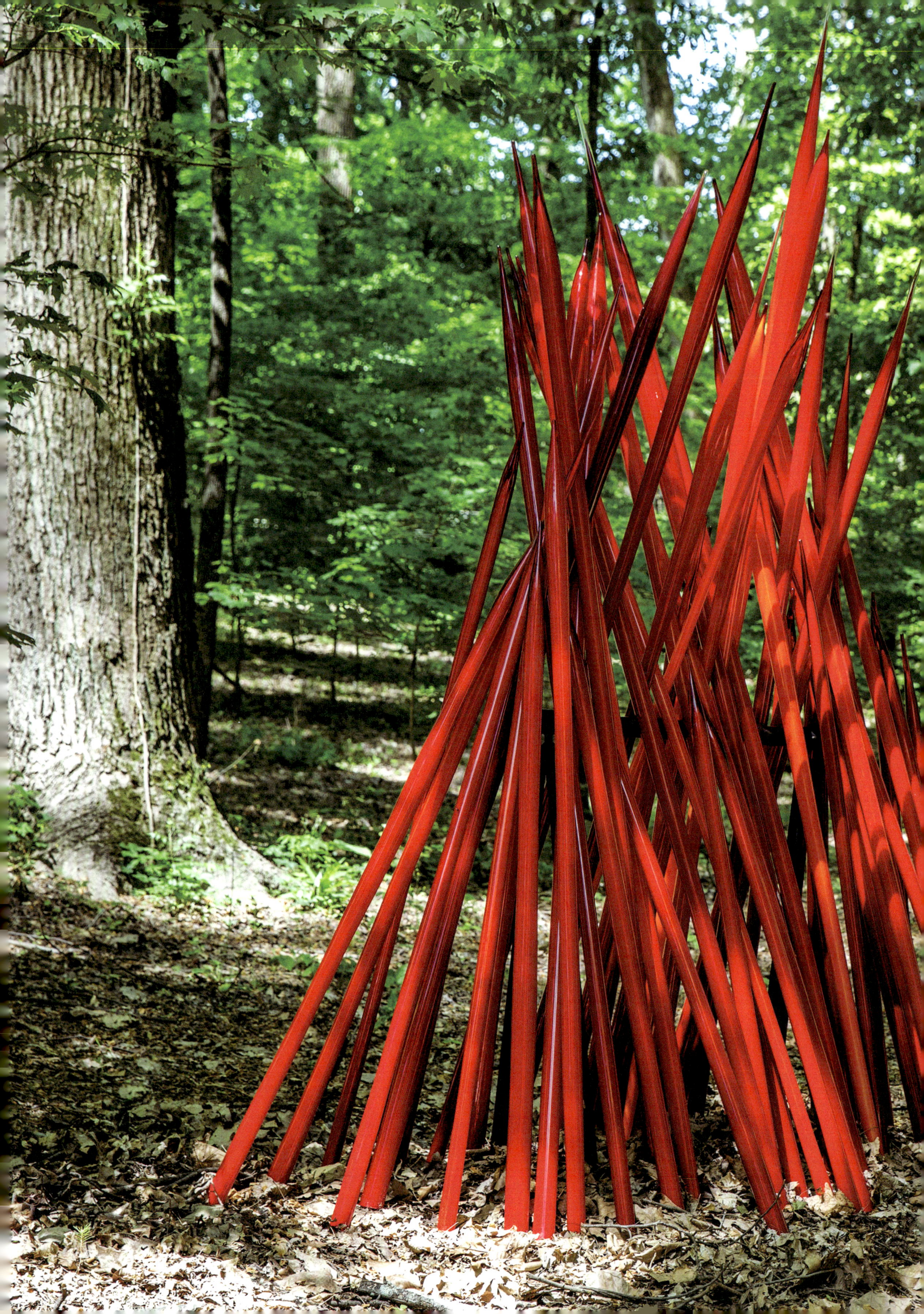

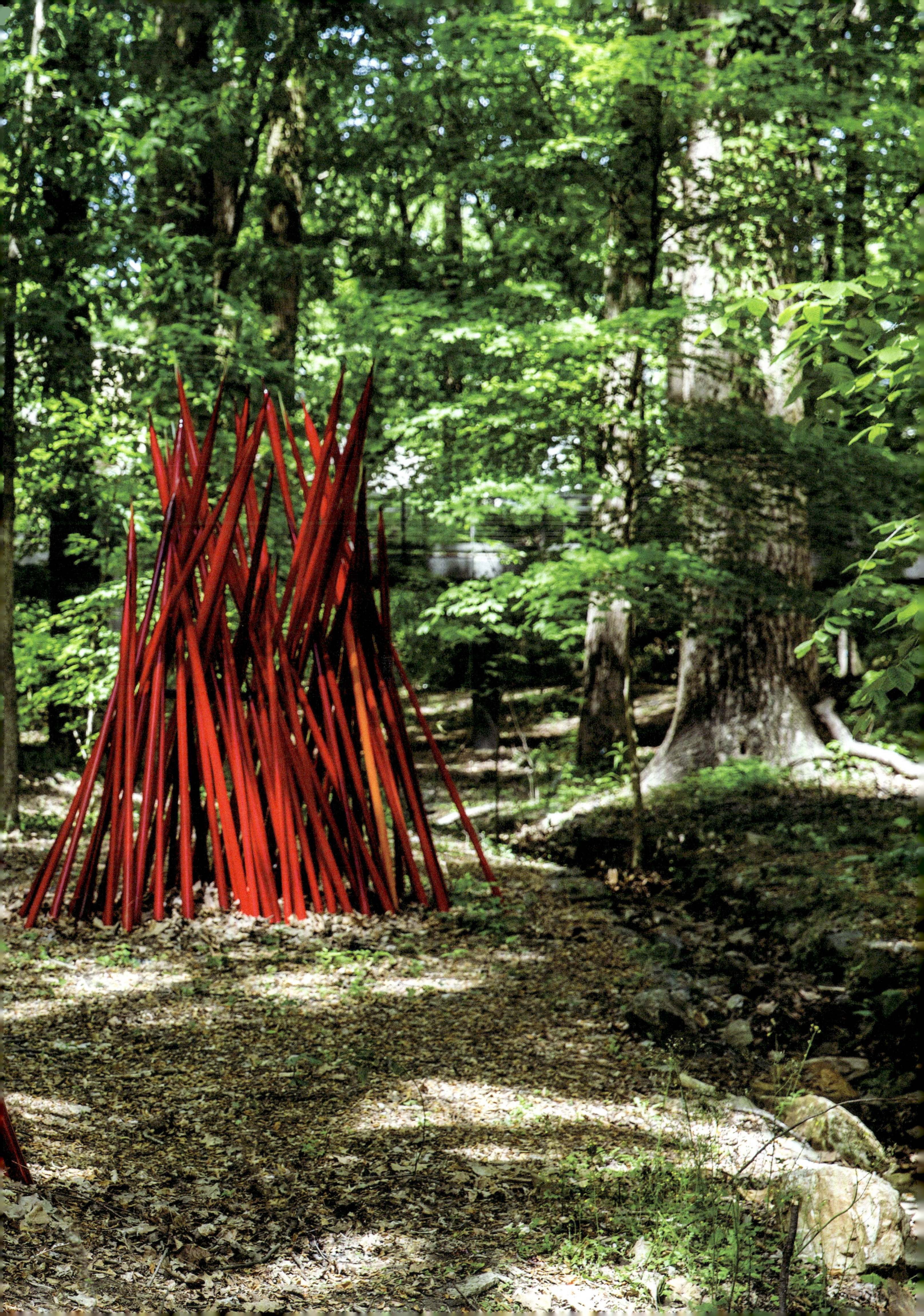

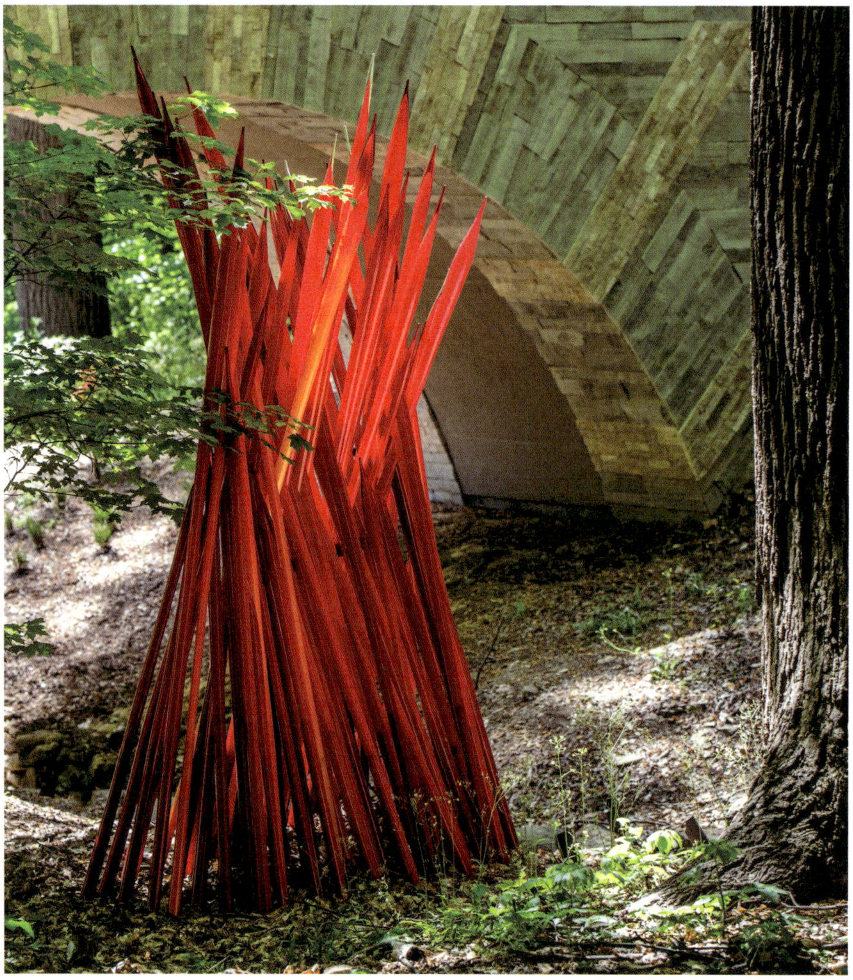

*Previous and above (detail opposite)*
**RED REEDS**
2014, installed 2016

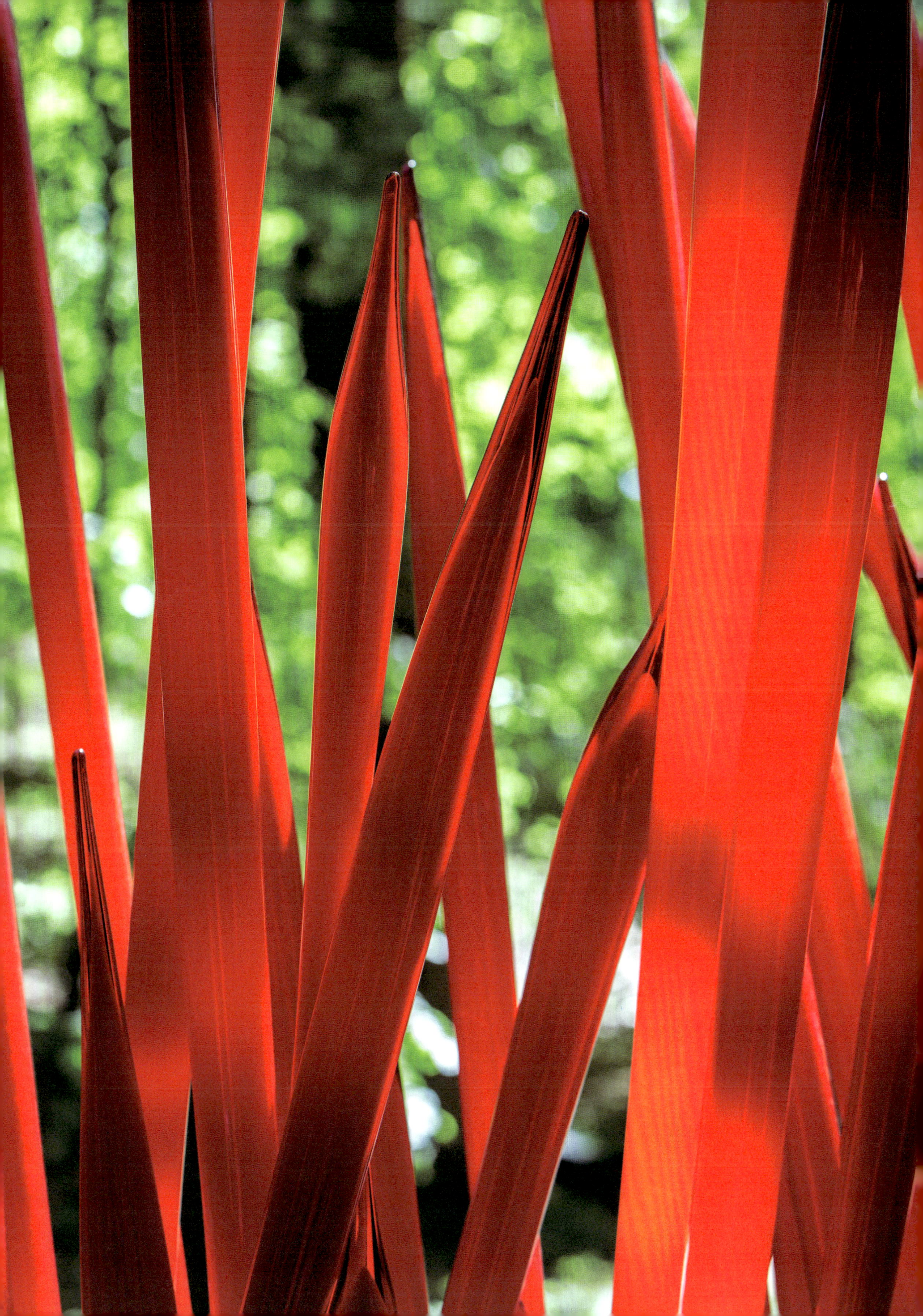

*Opposite and next*
**SAFFRON TOWER**
2008, 30 x 6 x 6'
installed 2016

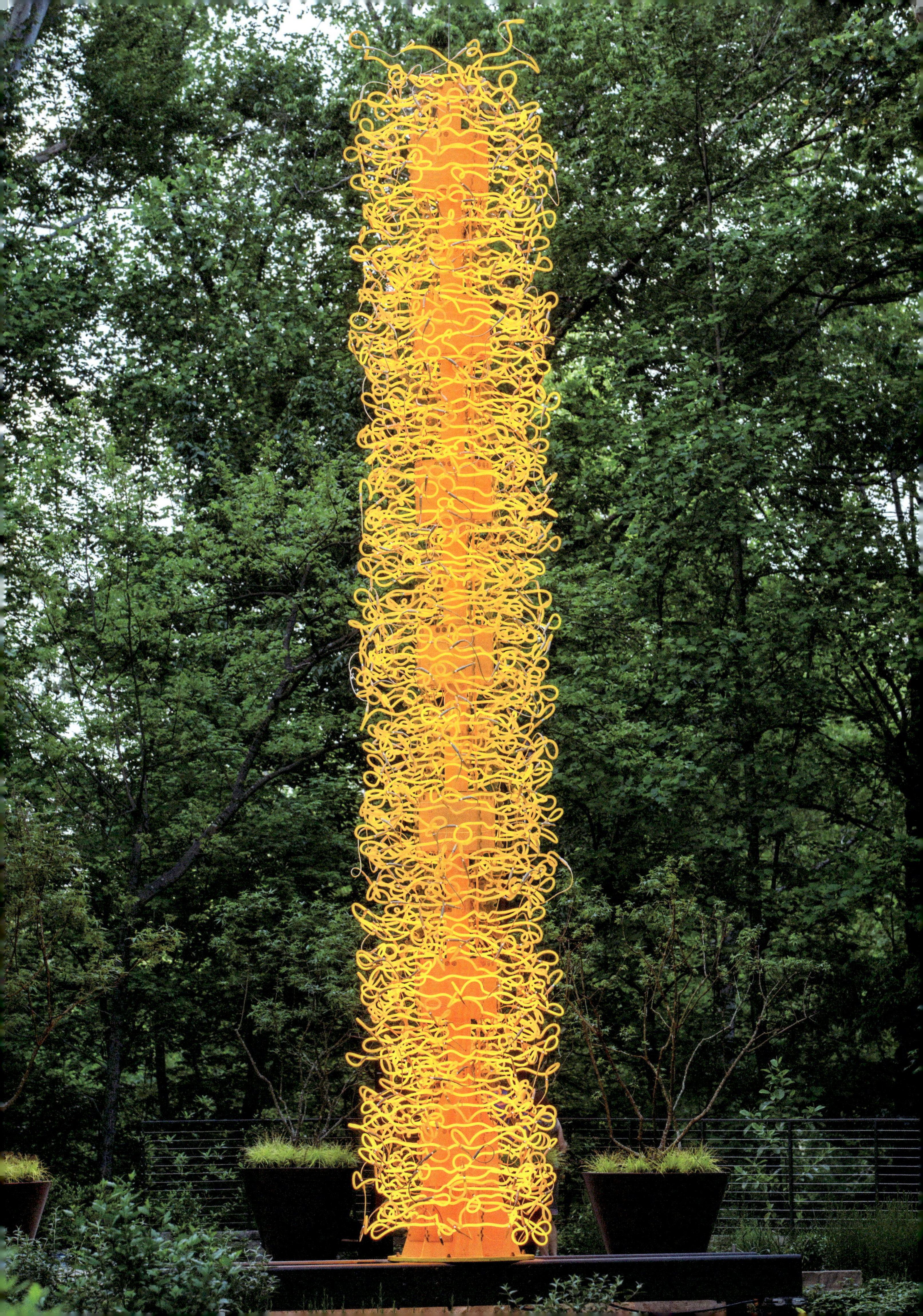

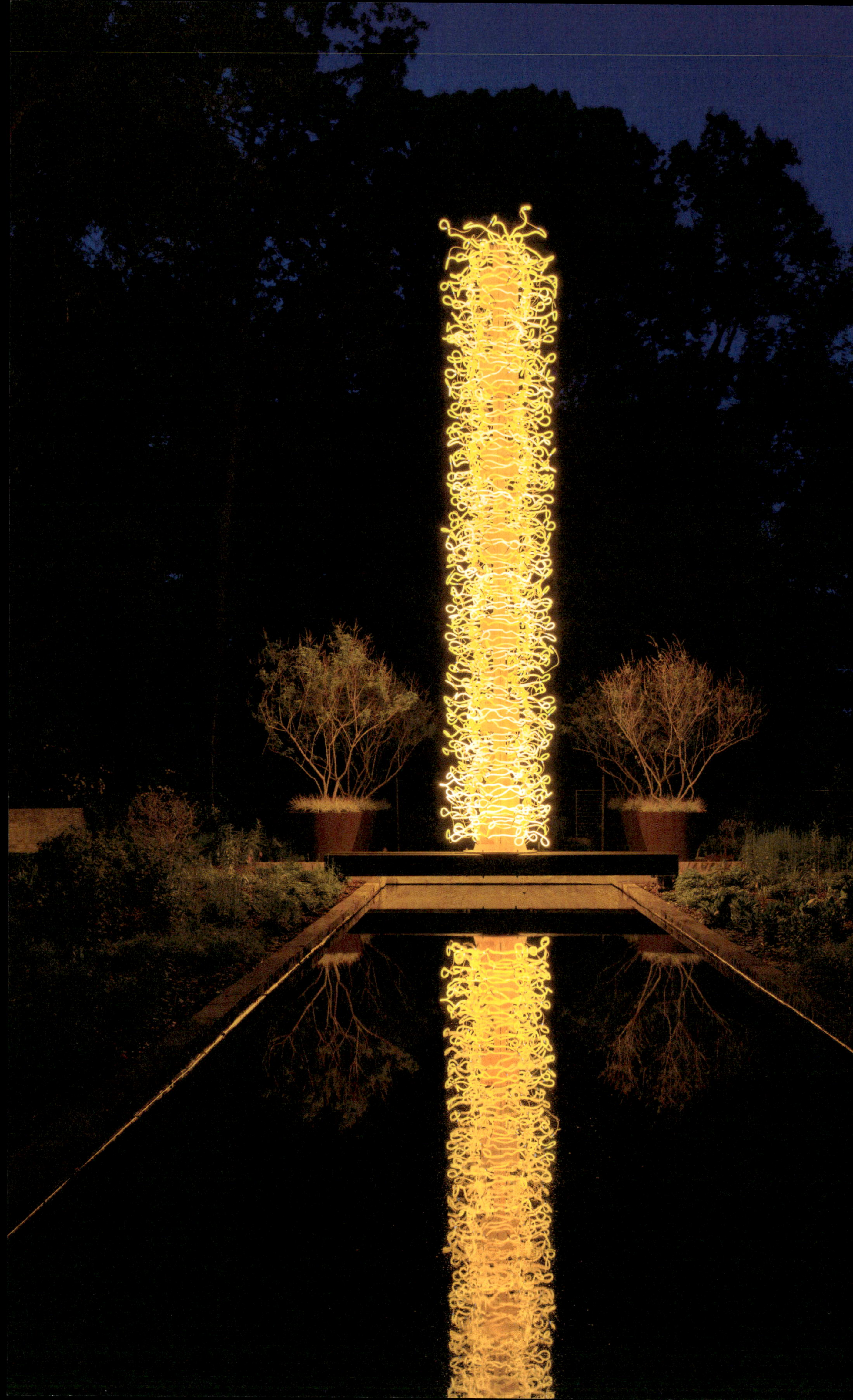

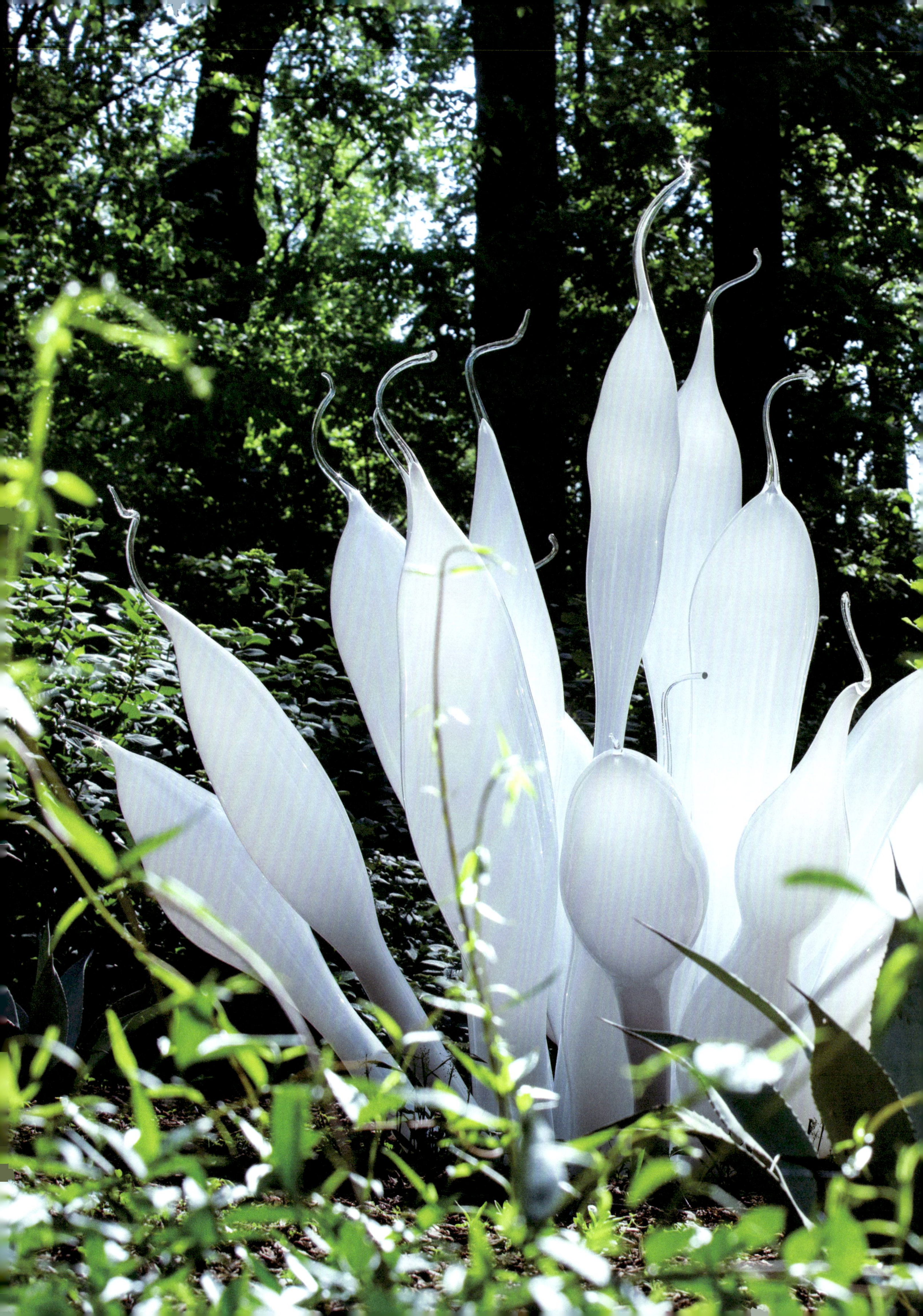

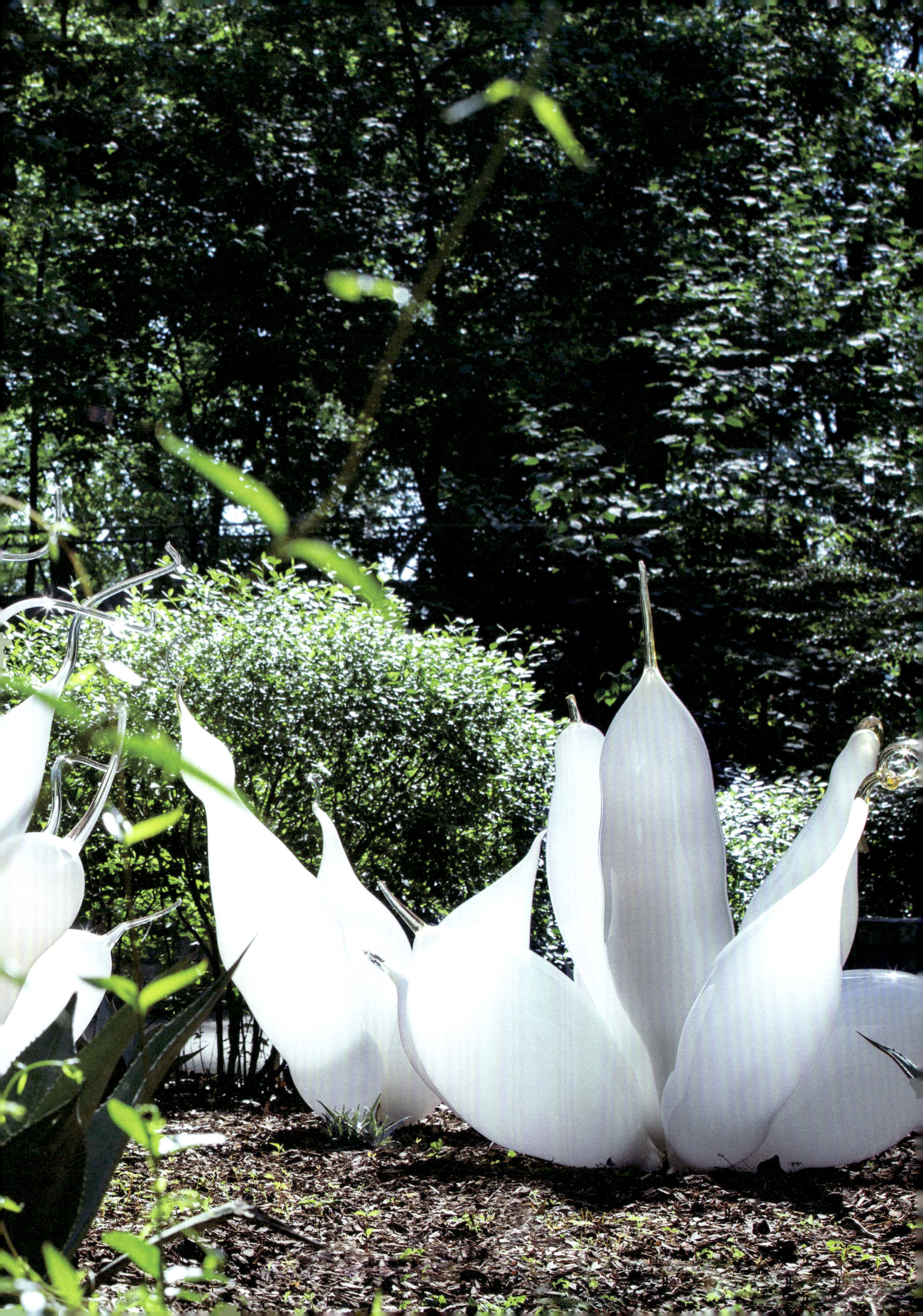

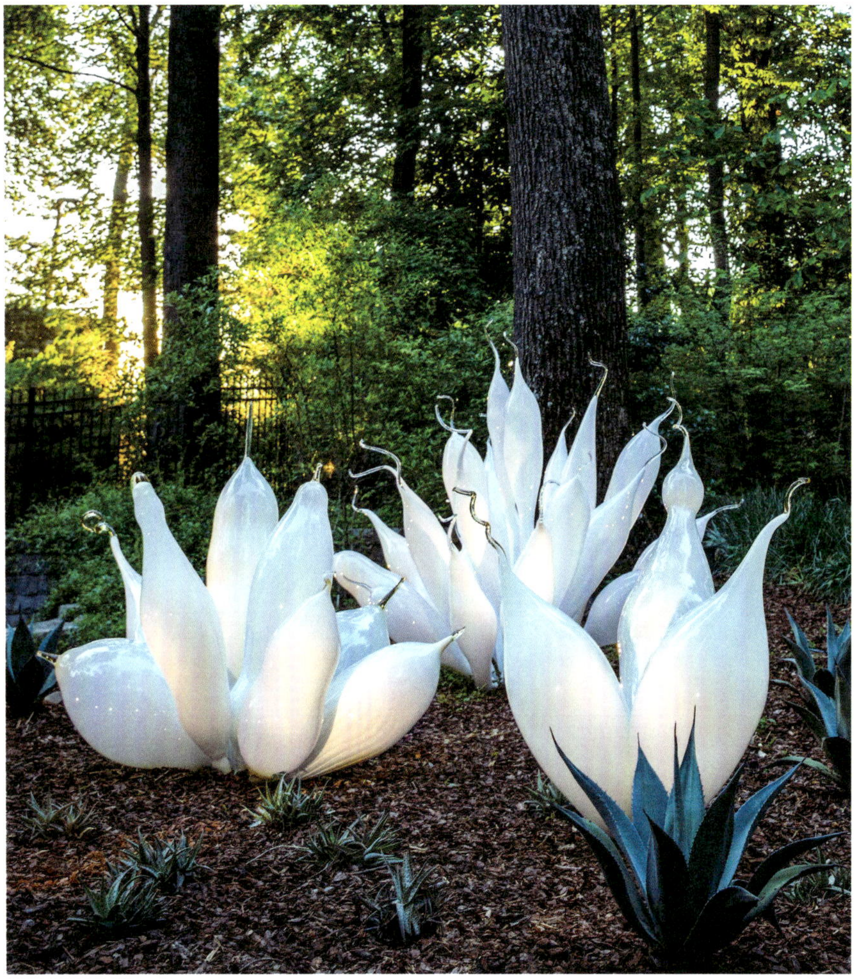

*Previous and above (detail opposite)*
**WHITE BELUGAS**
2014, installed 2016

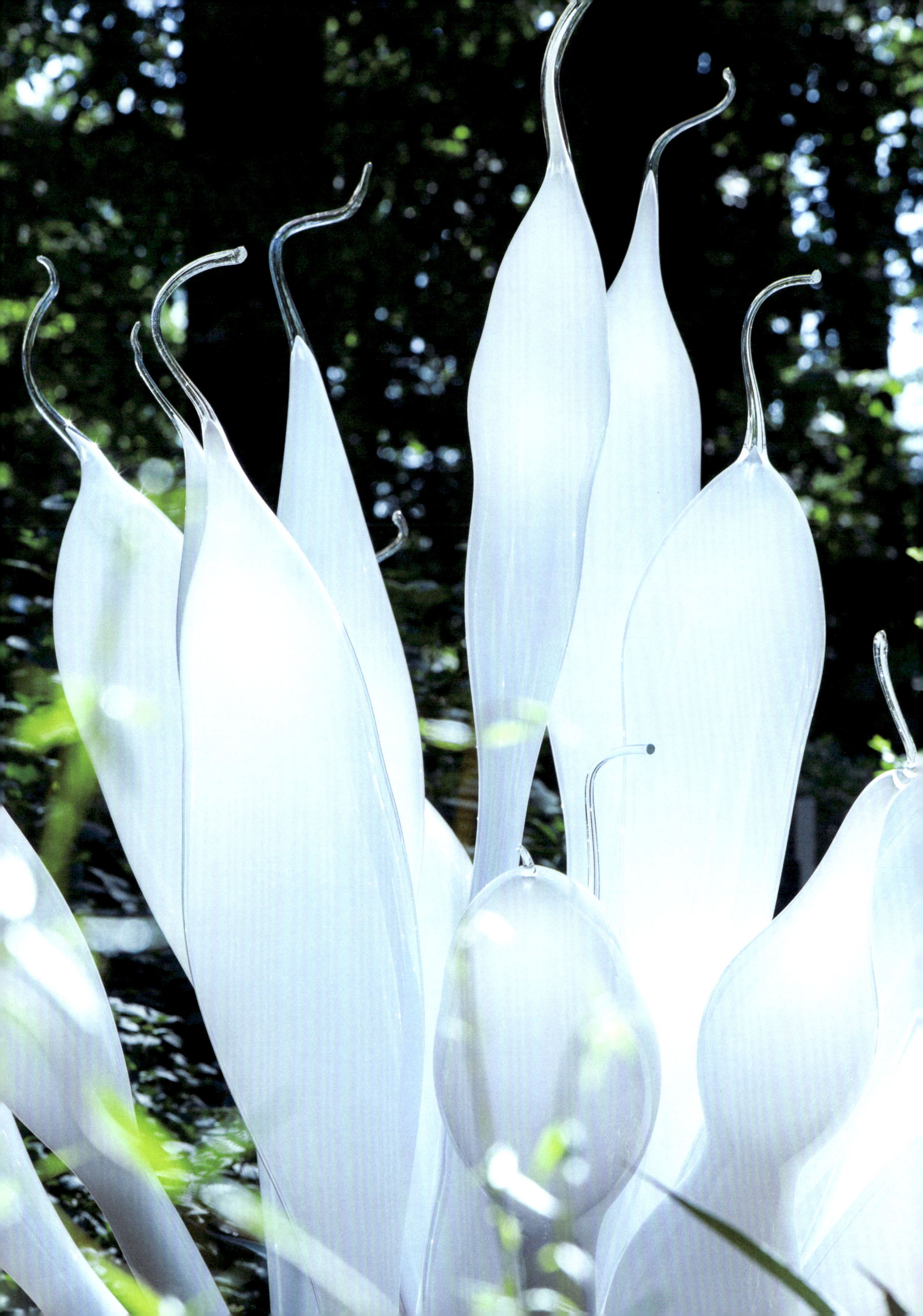

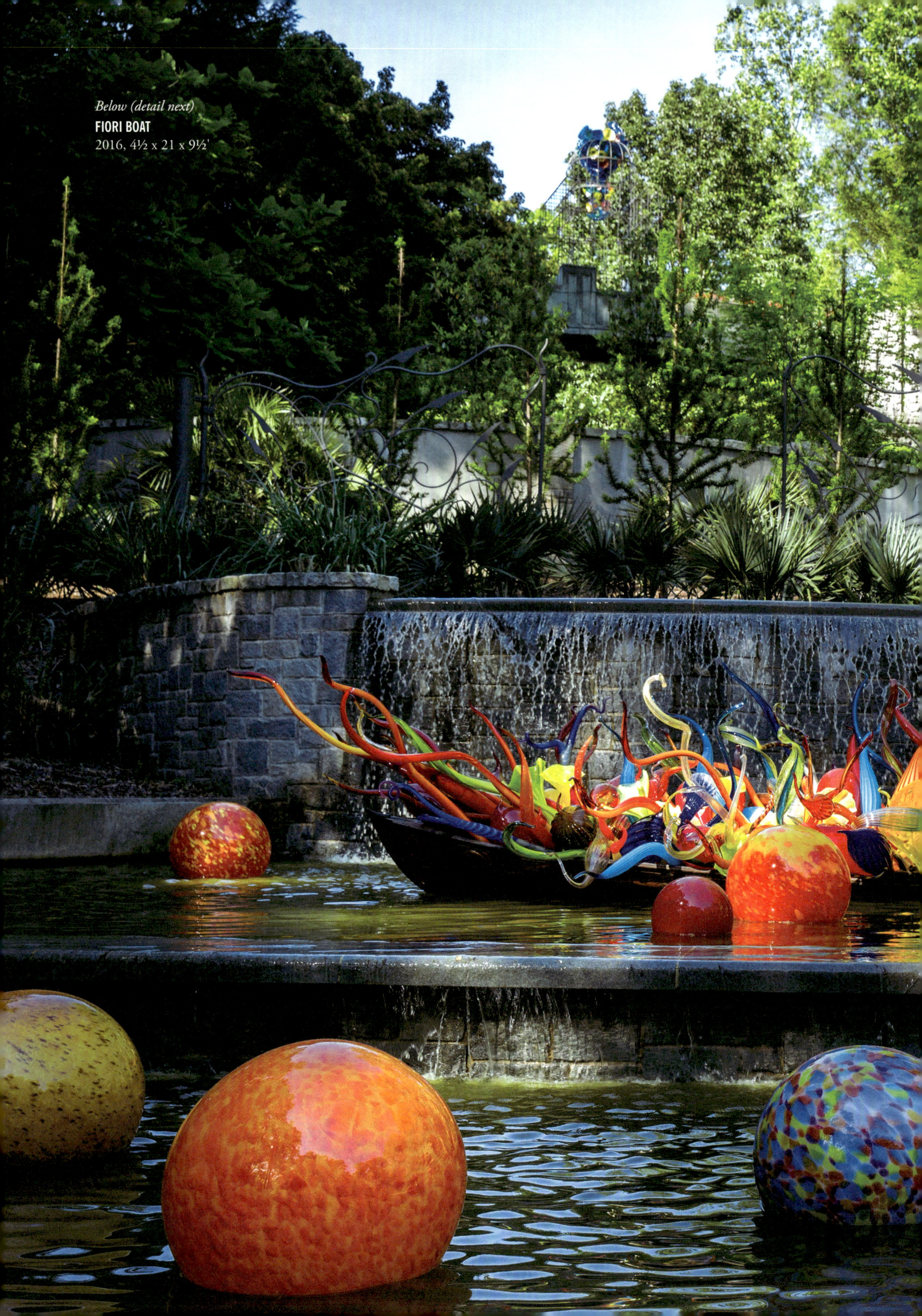

*Below (detail next)*
**FIORI BOAT**
2016, 4½ x 21 x 9½'

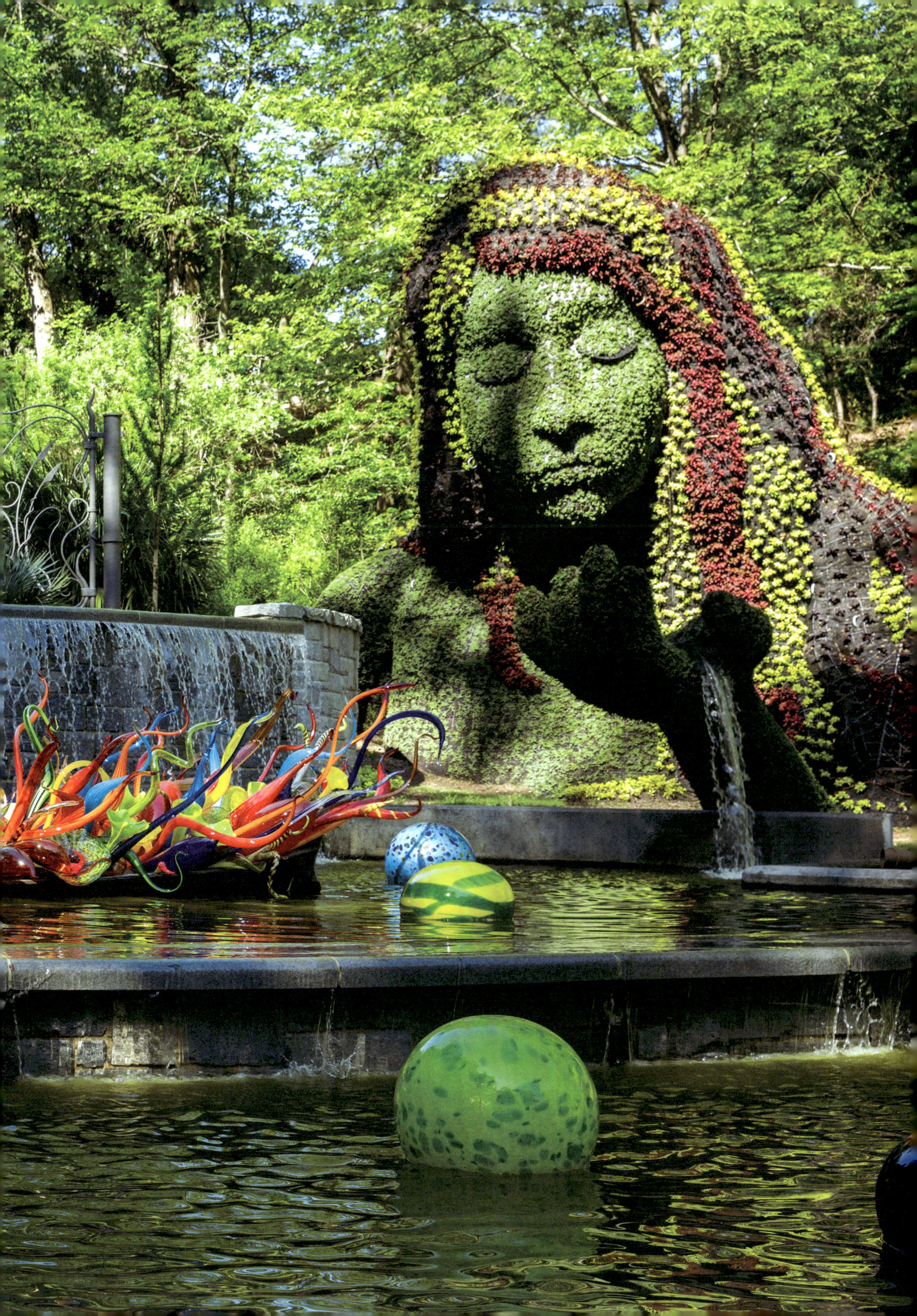

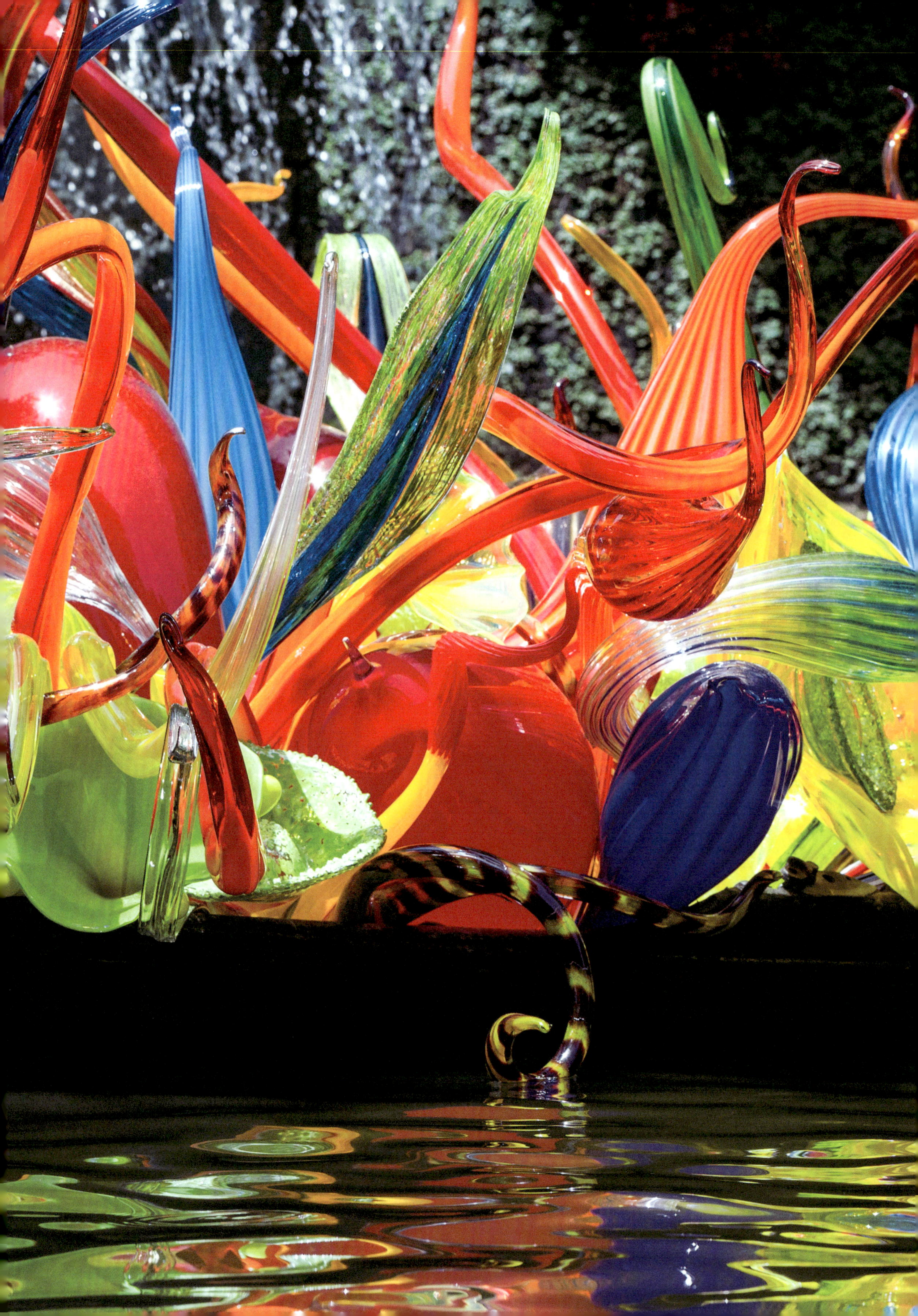

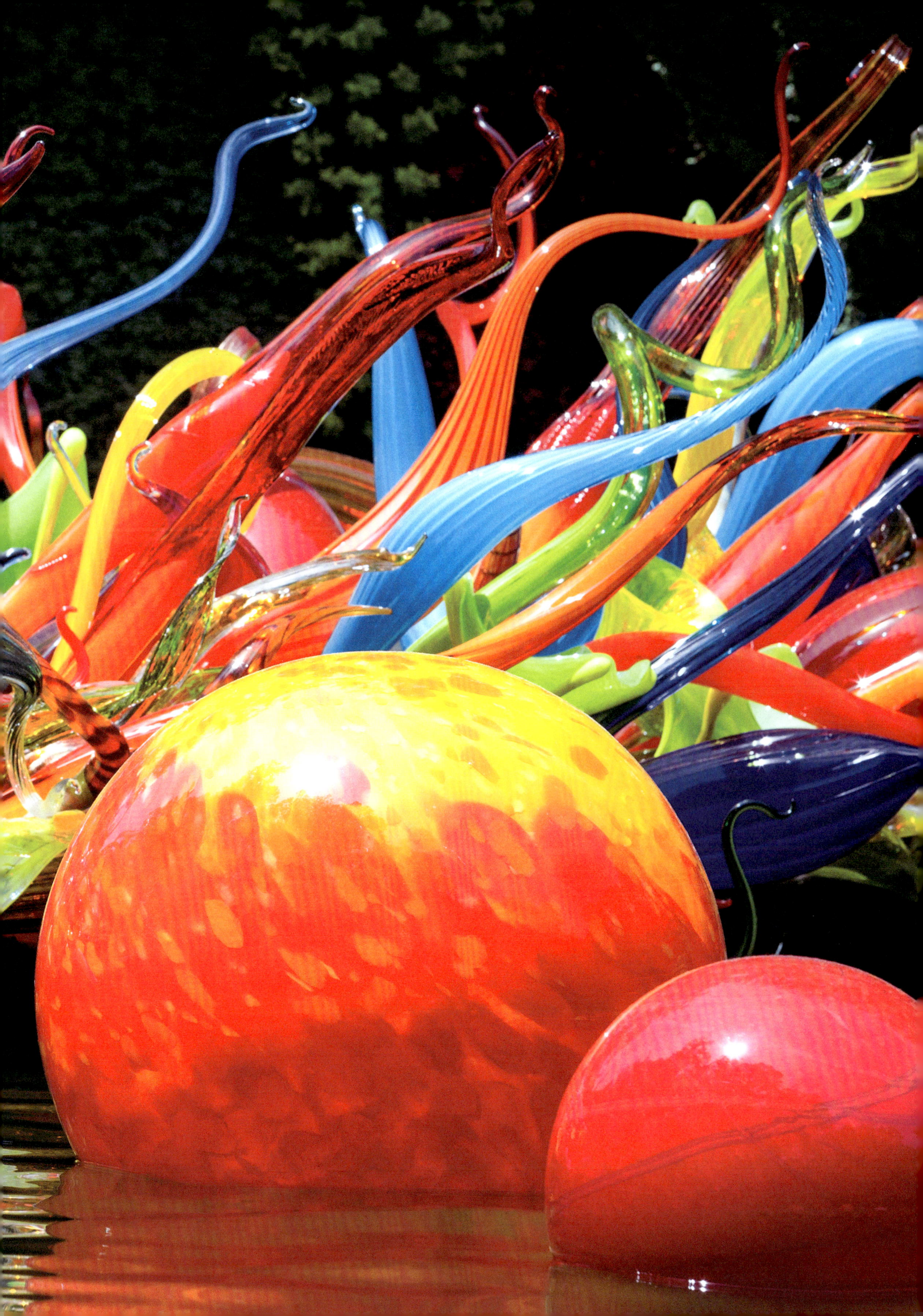

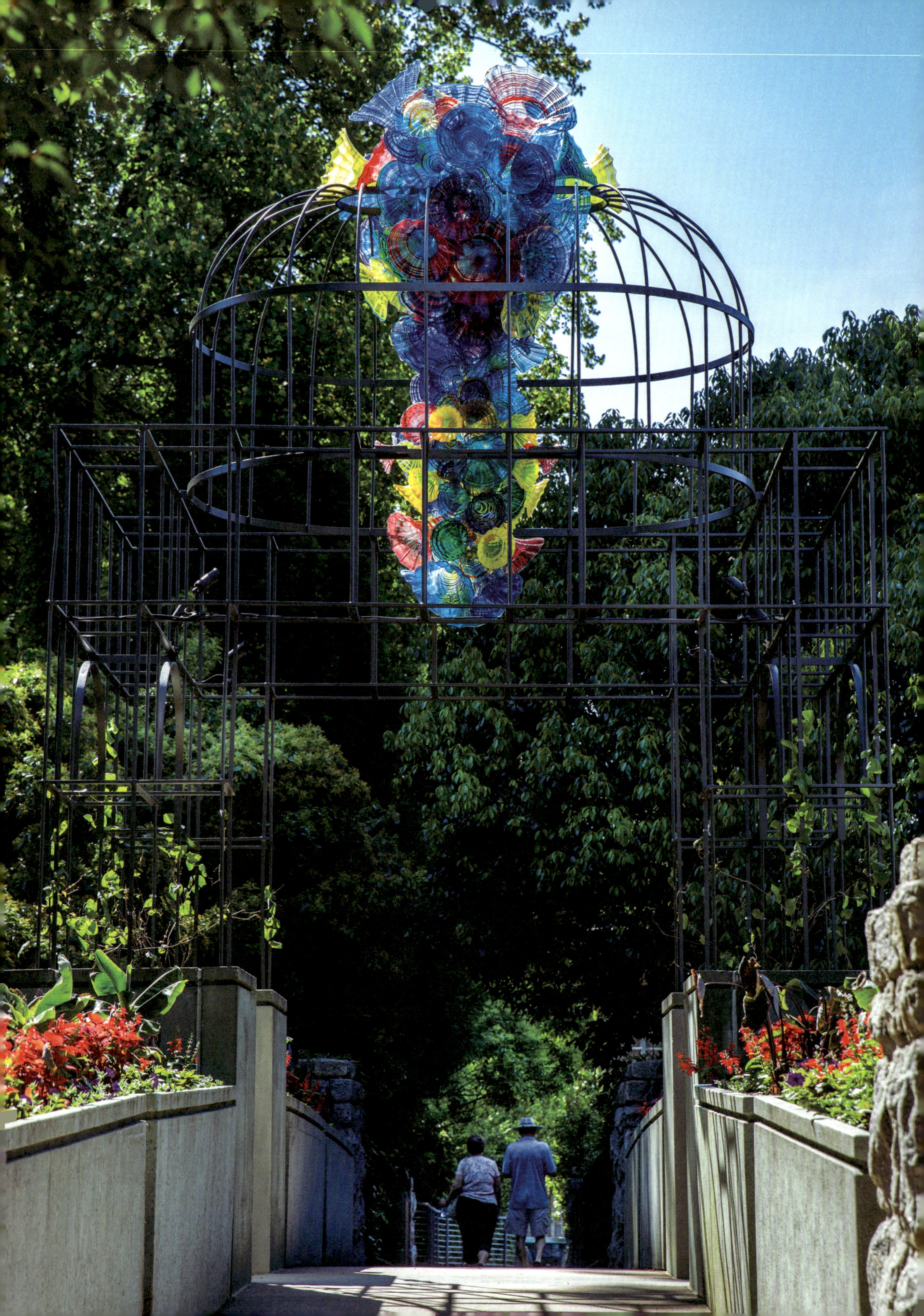

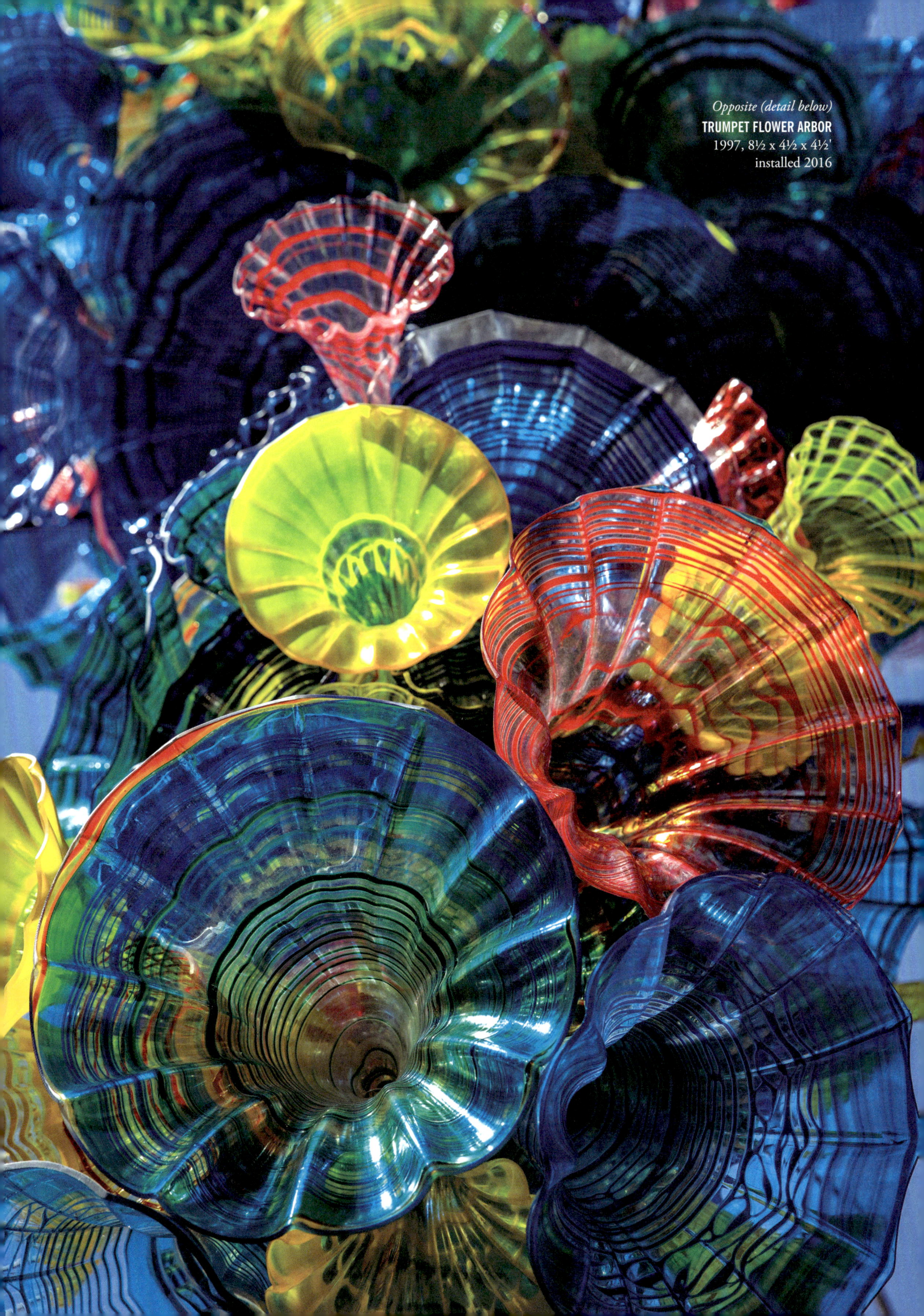

*Opposite (detail below)*
**TRUMPET FLOWER ARBOR**
1997, 8½ x 4½ x 4½'
installed 2016

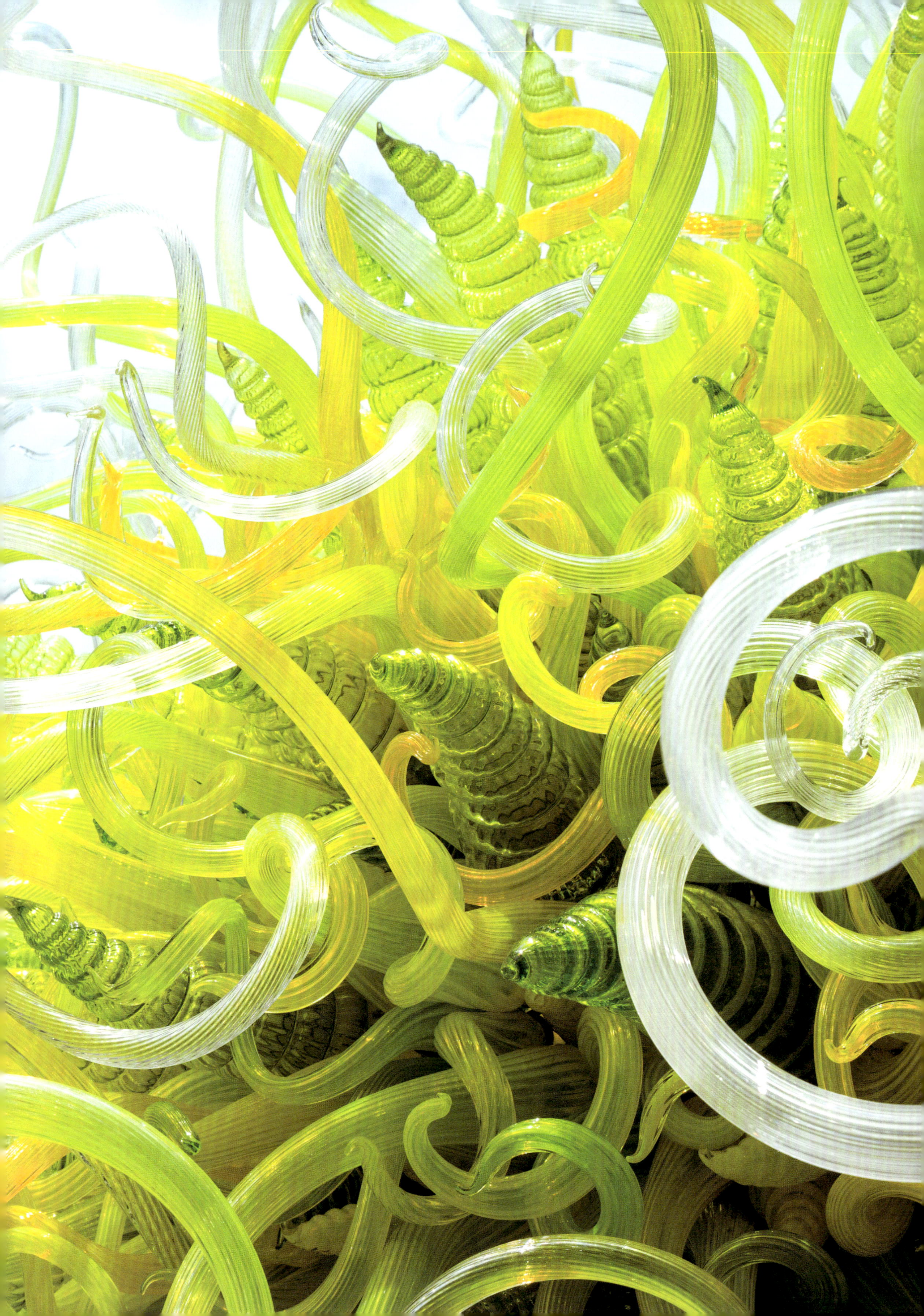

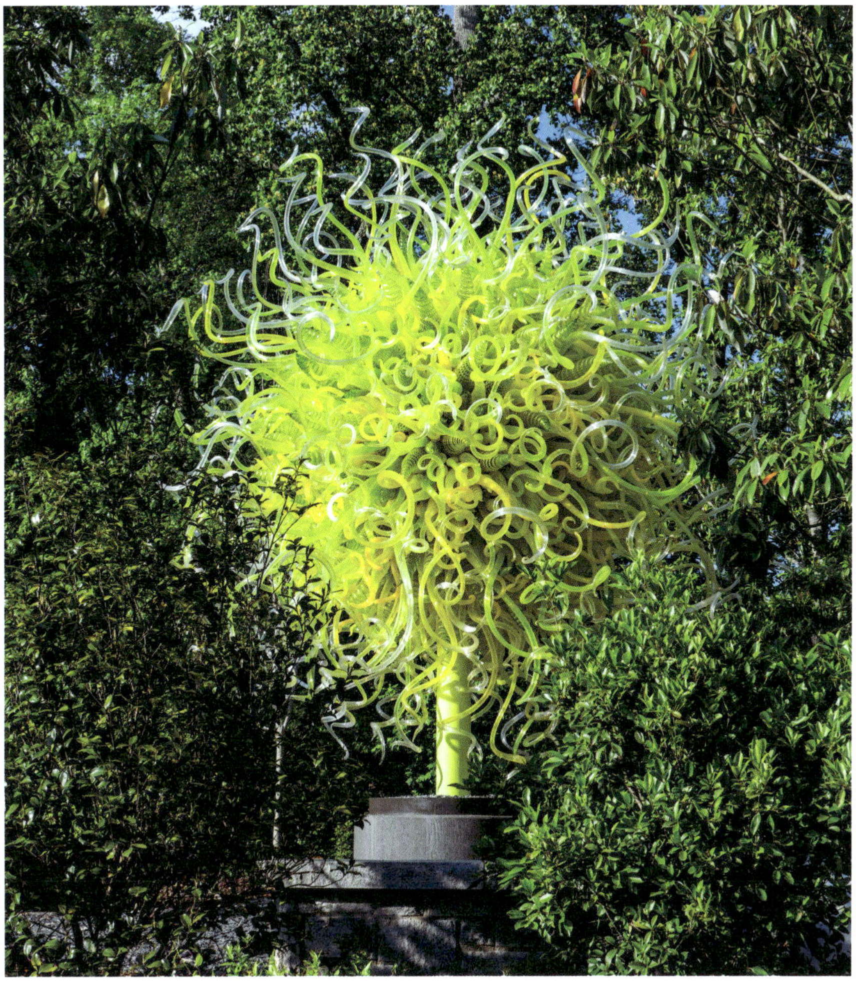

*Above and next (detail opposite)*

**SOL DEL CITRÓN**

2014, 13½ x 13½ x 13'

installed 2016

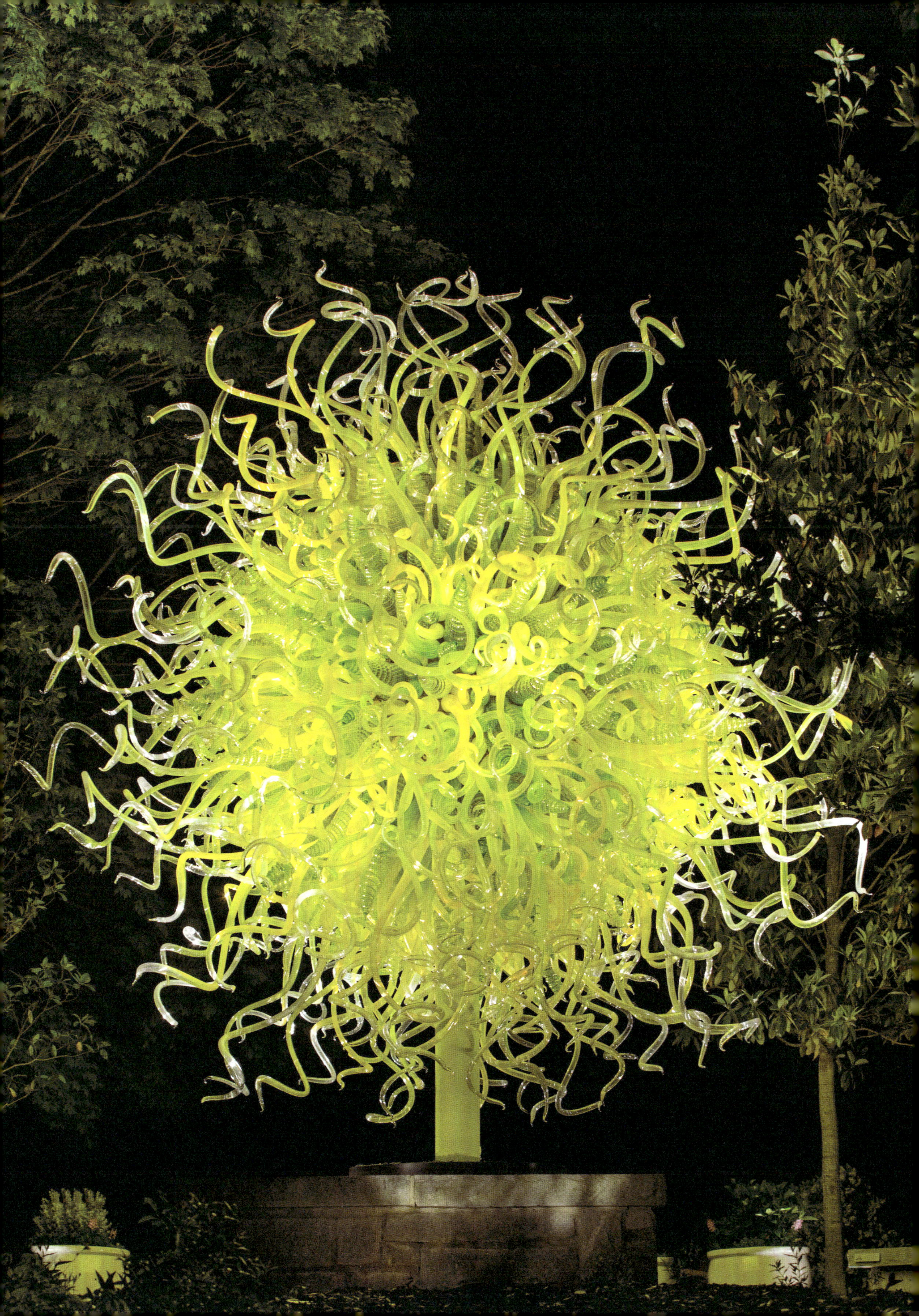

*Opposite (detail next)*
**THREE GRACES TOWER**
2016, 84 x 96 x 96"

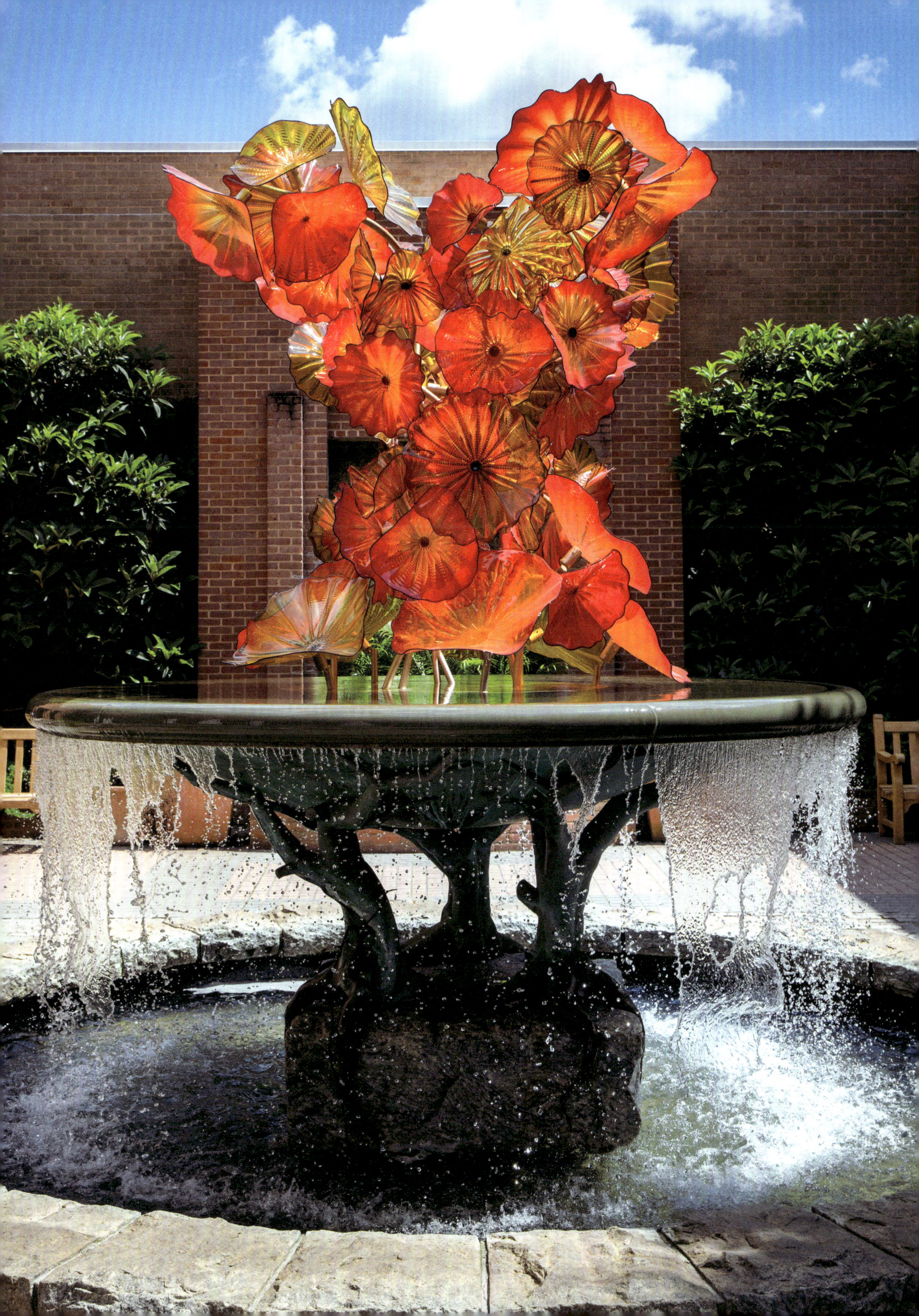

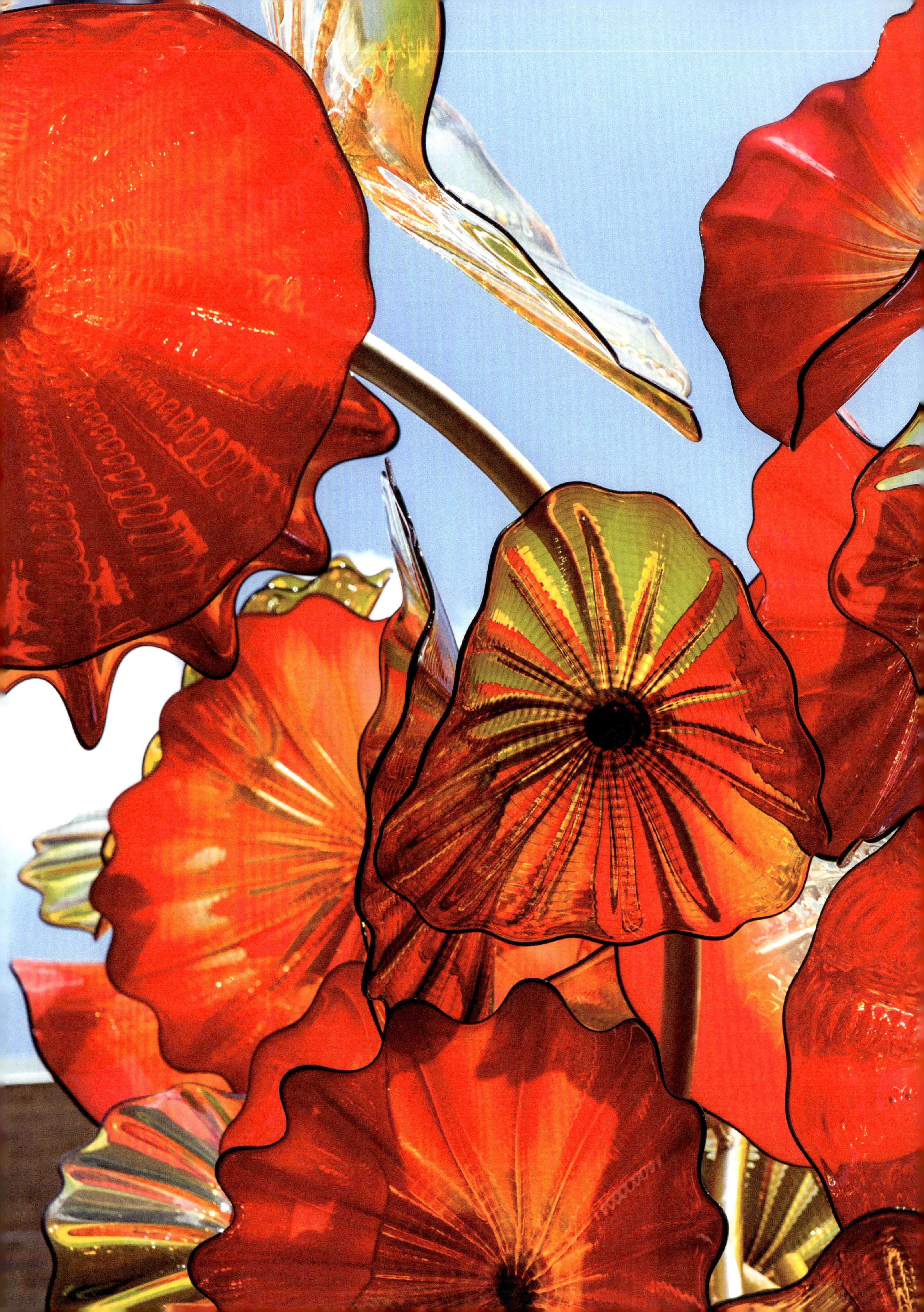

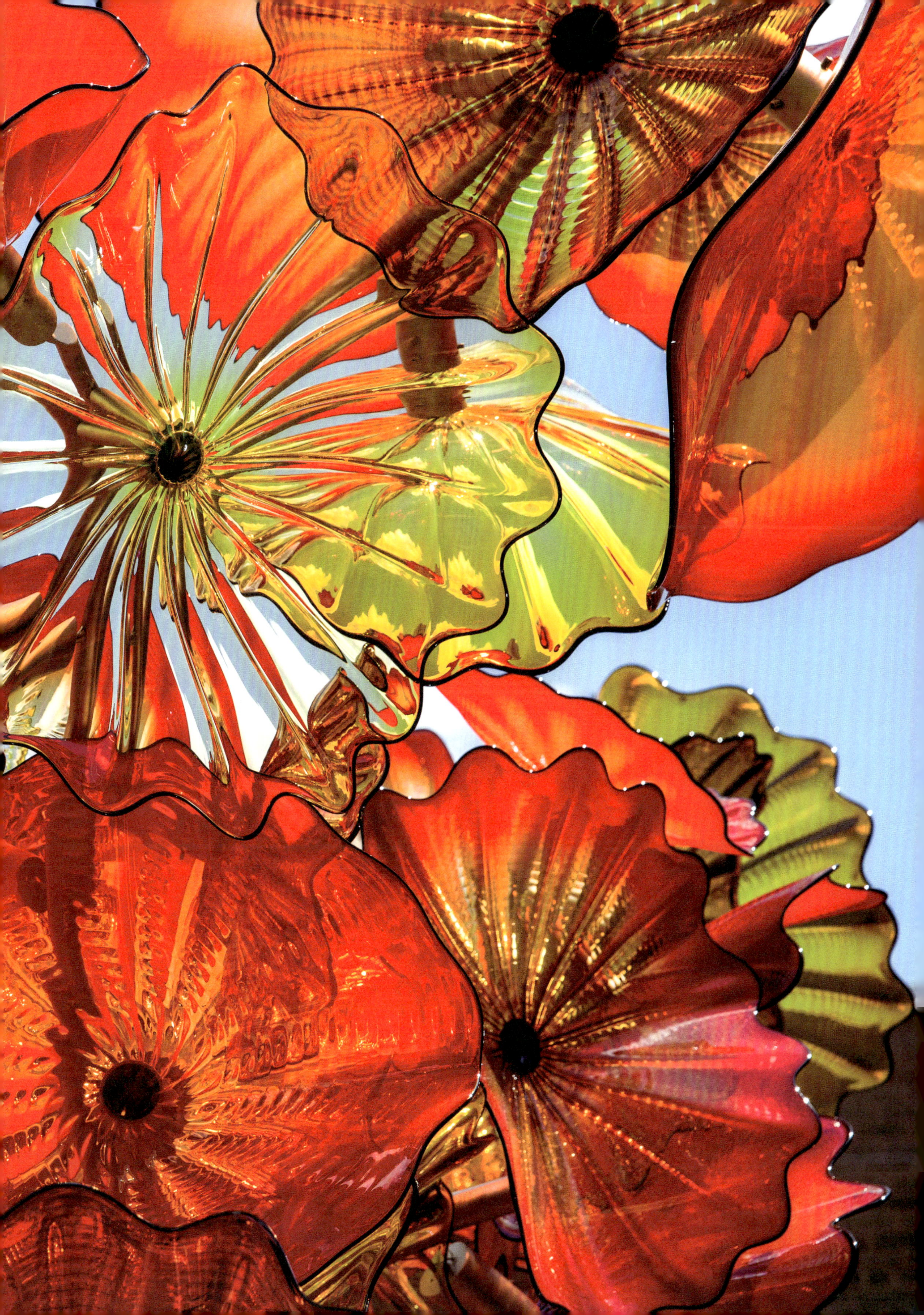

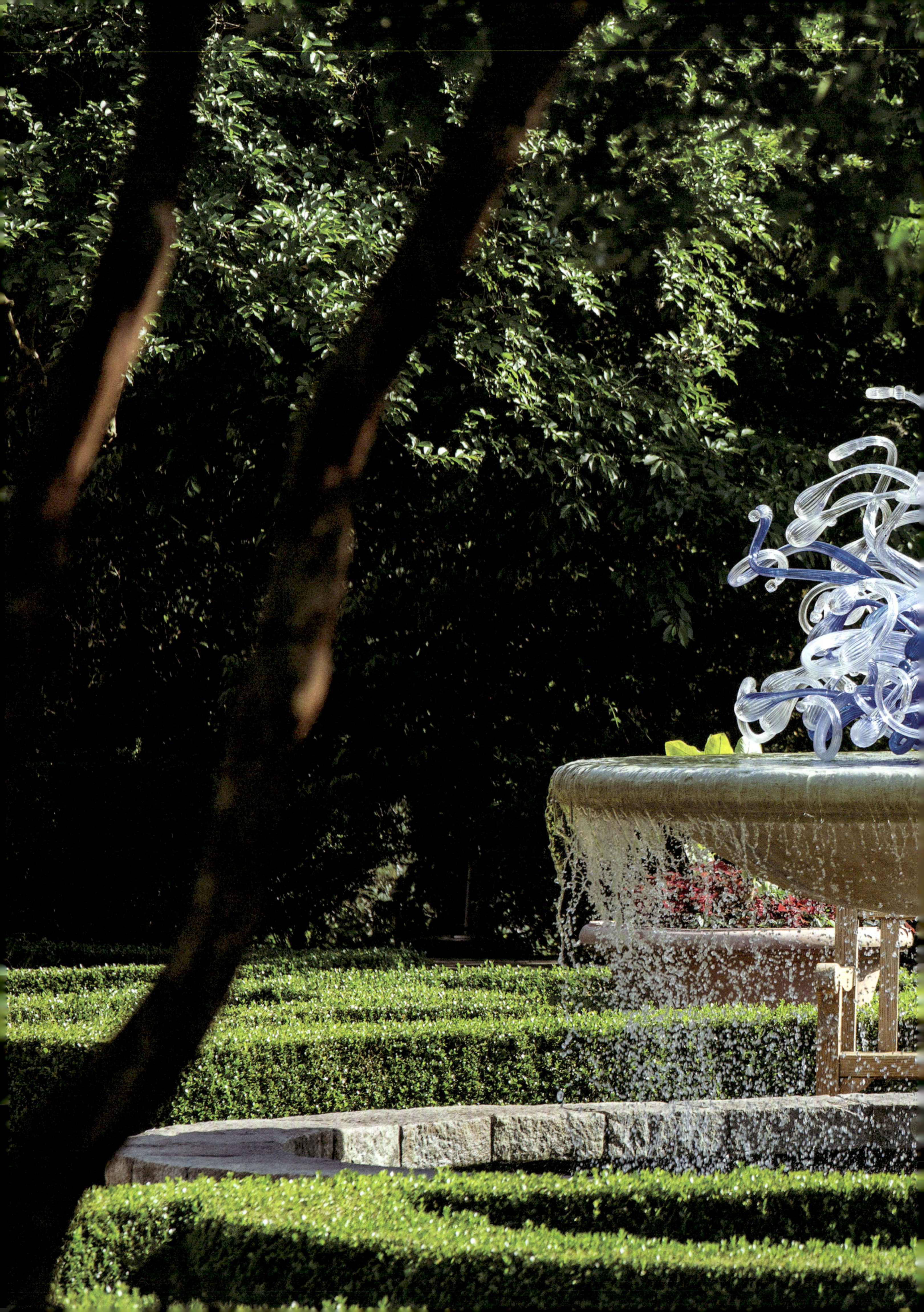

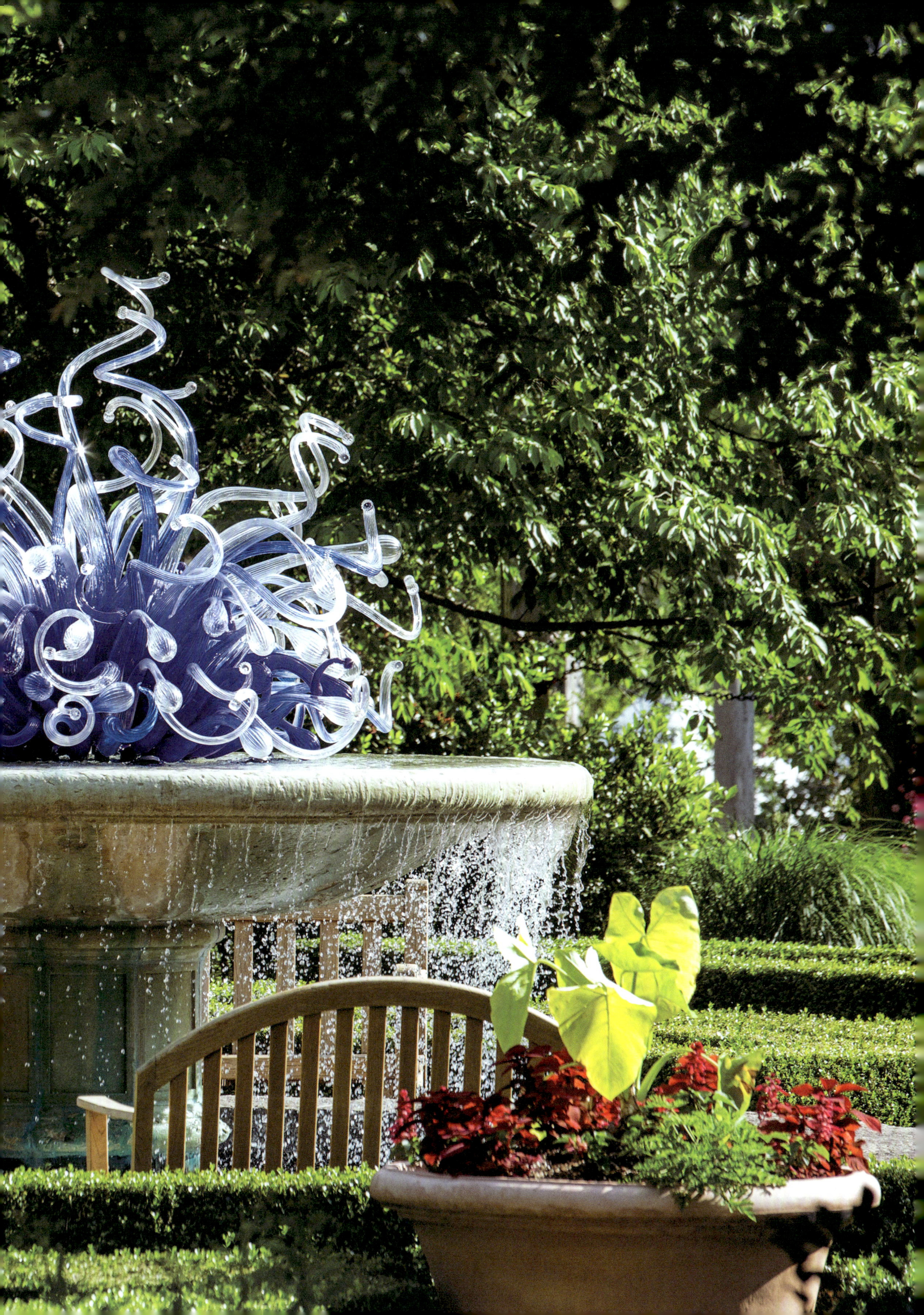

*Previous*
**PARTERRE FOUNTAIN**
2004, 54 x 92 x 95"

*Opposite*
**TURQUOISE FLOATS**
2015, installed 2016

*Next*
**TURQUOISE MARLINS**
2015, installed 2016

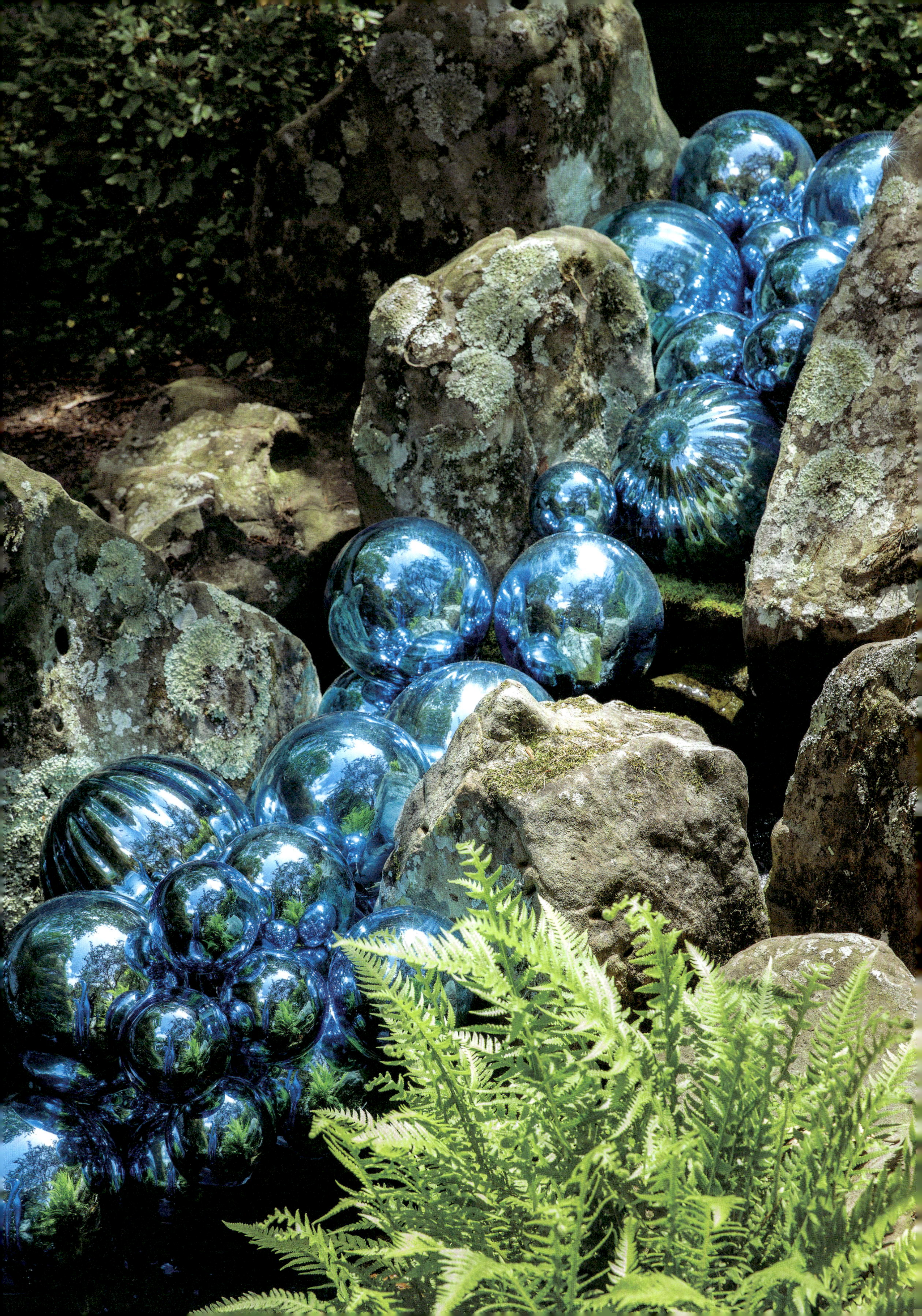

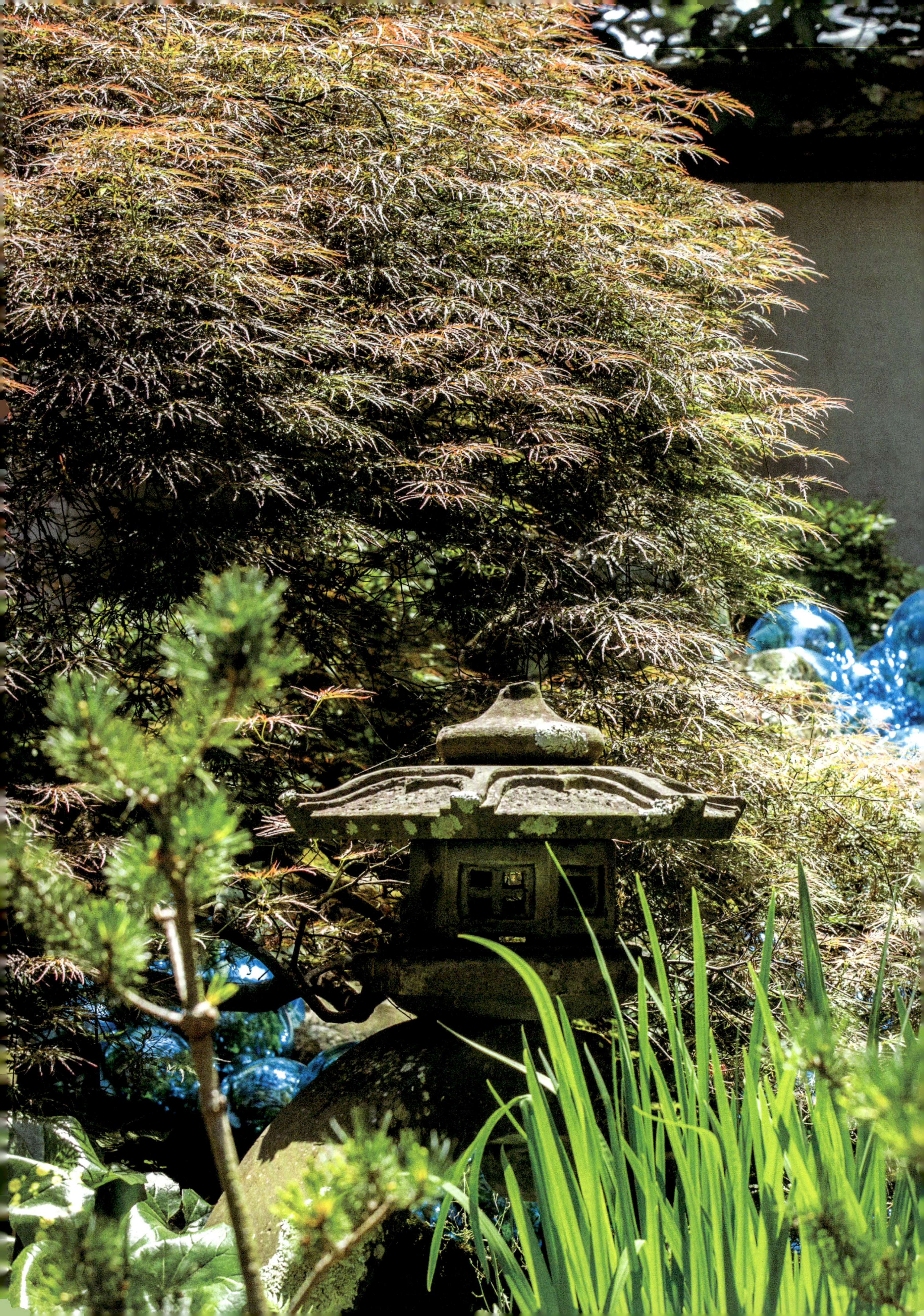

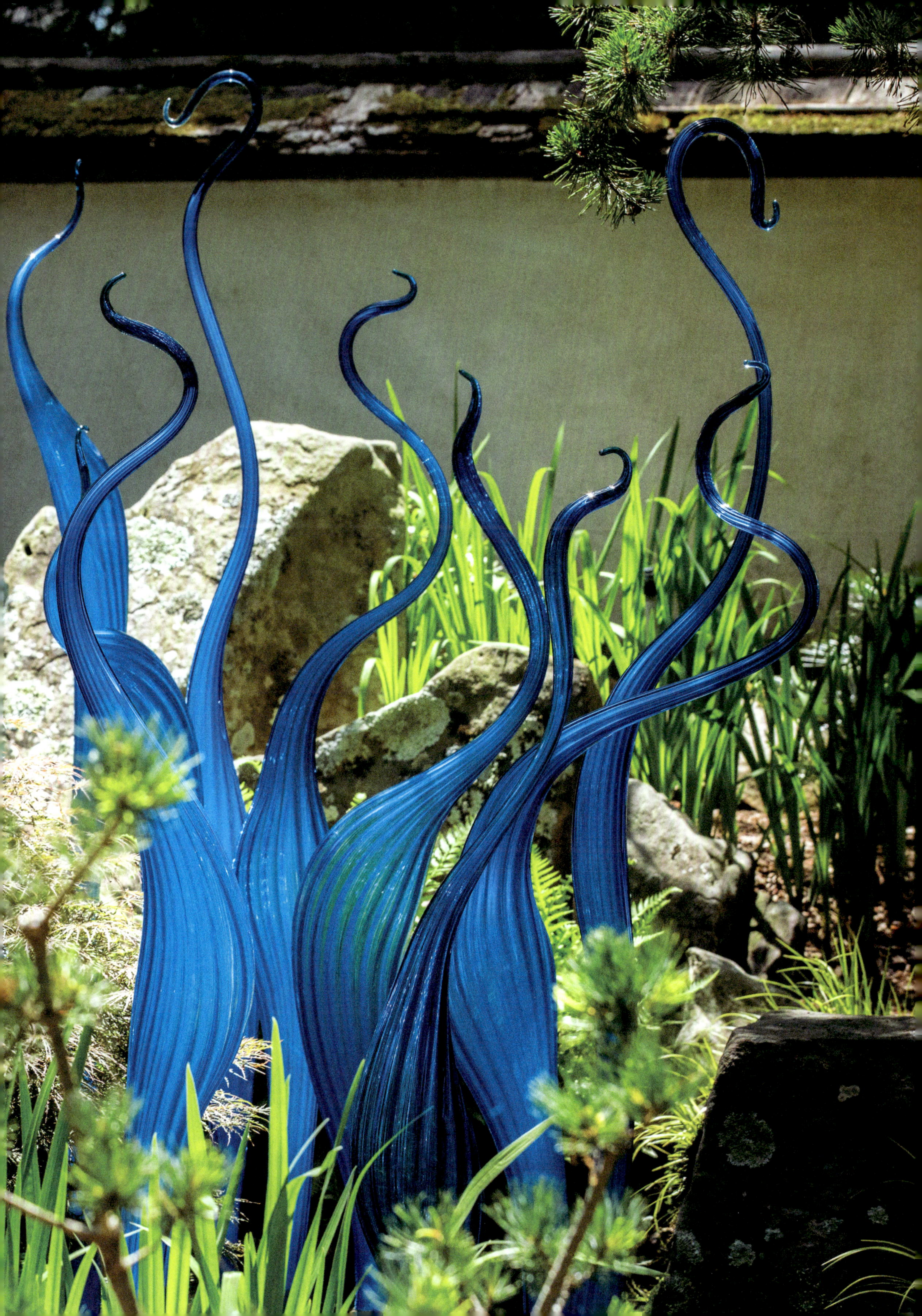

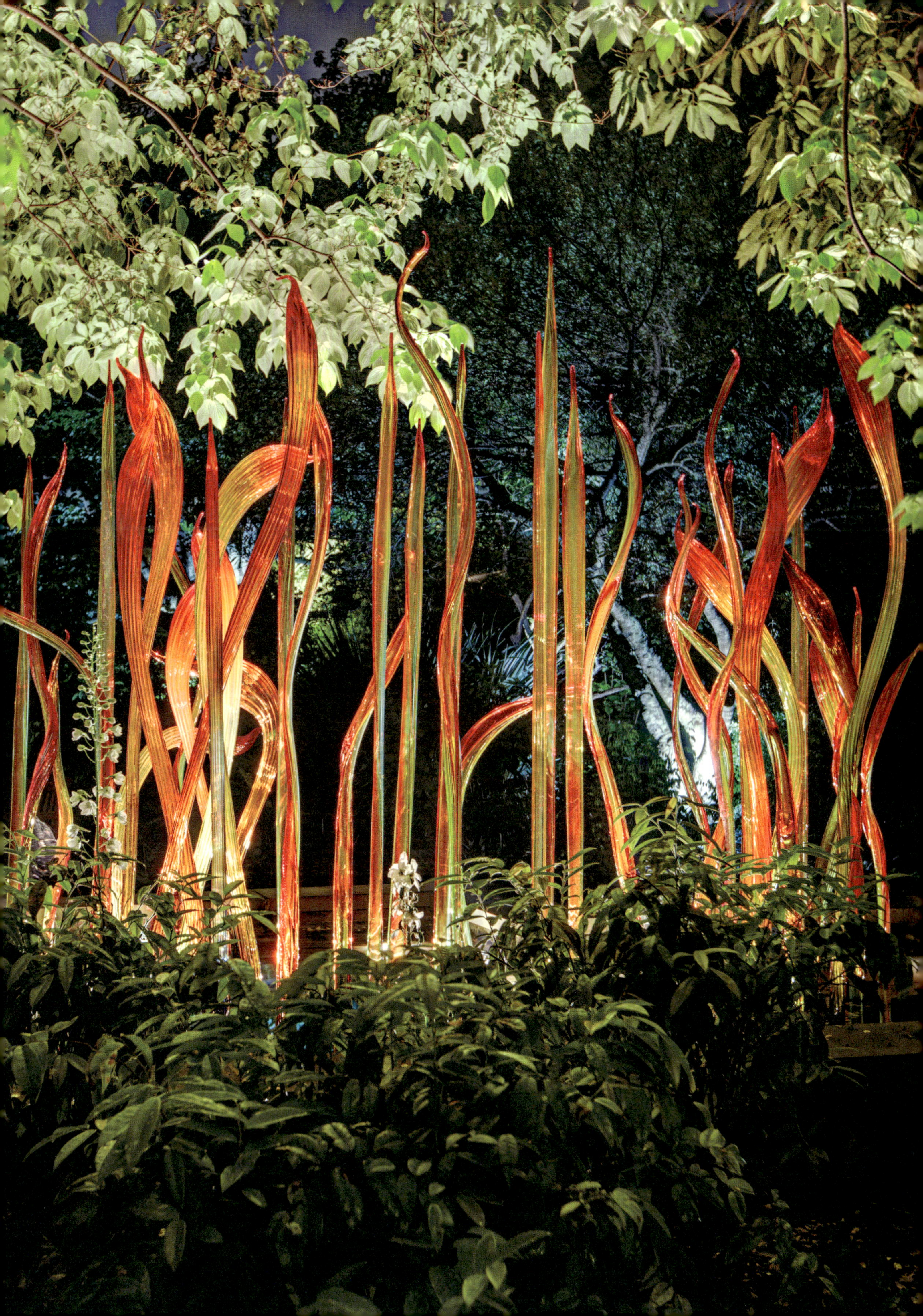

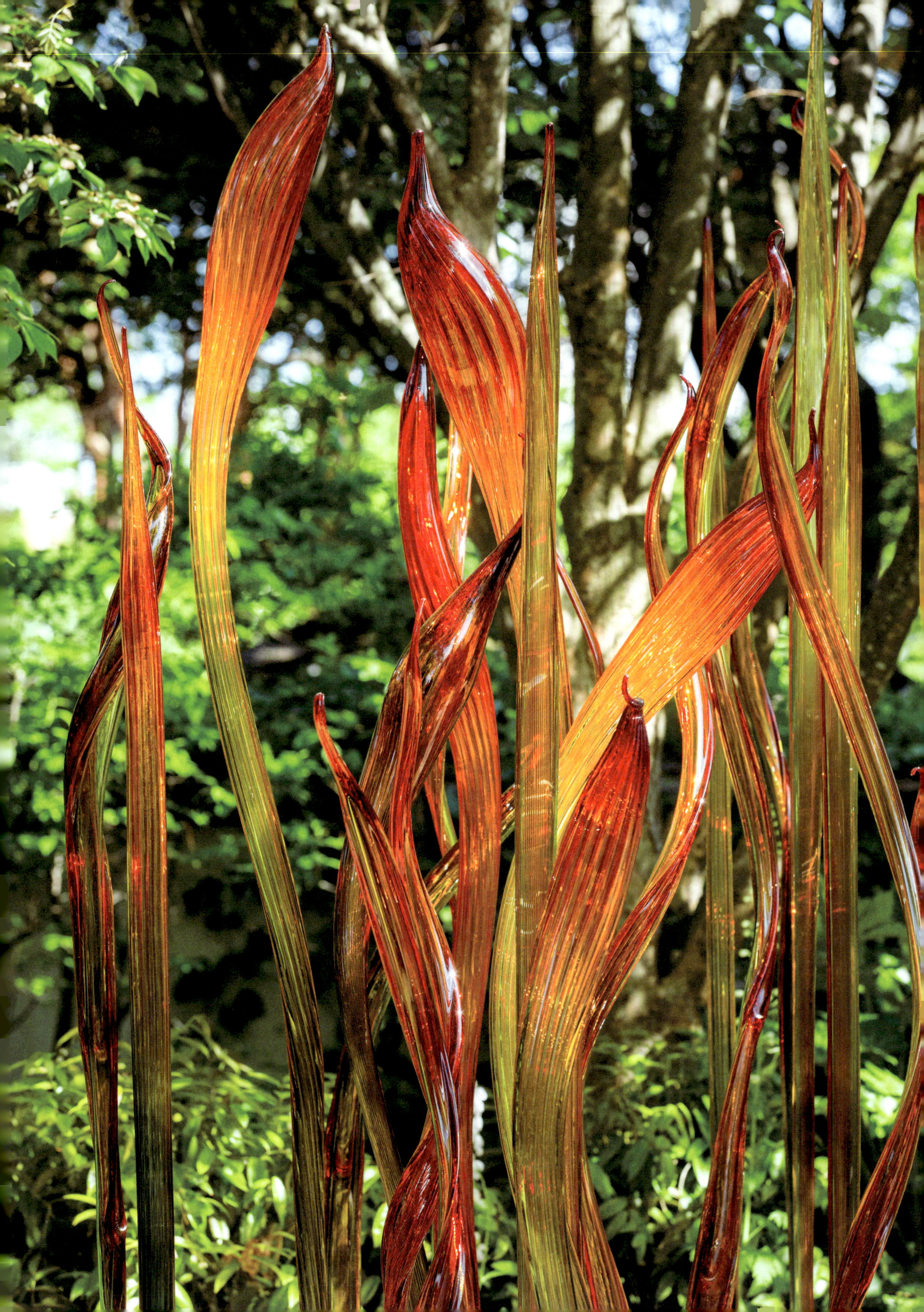

*Previous (detail opposite)*
**FIRE AMBER HERONS**
2016, 8 x 10 x 7'

*Opposite and next (detail next)*
**SAPPHIRE STAR**
2010, 92 x 93 x 92"
installed 2016

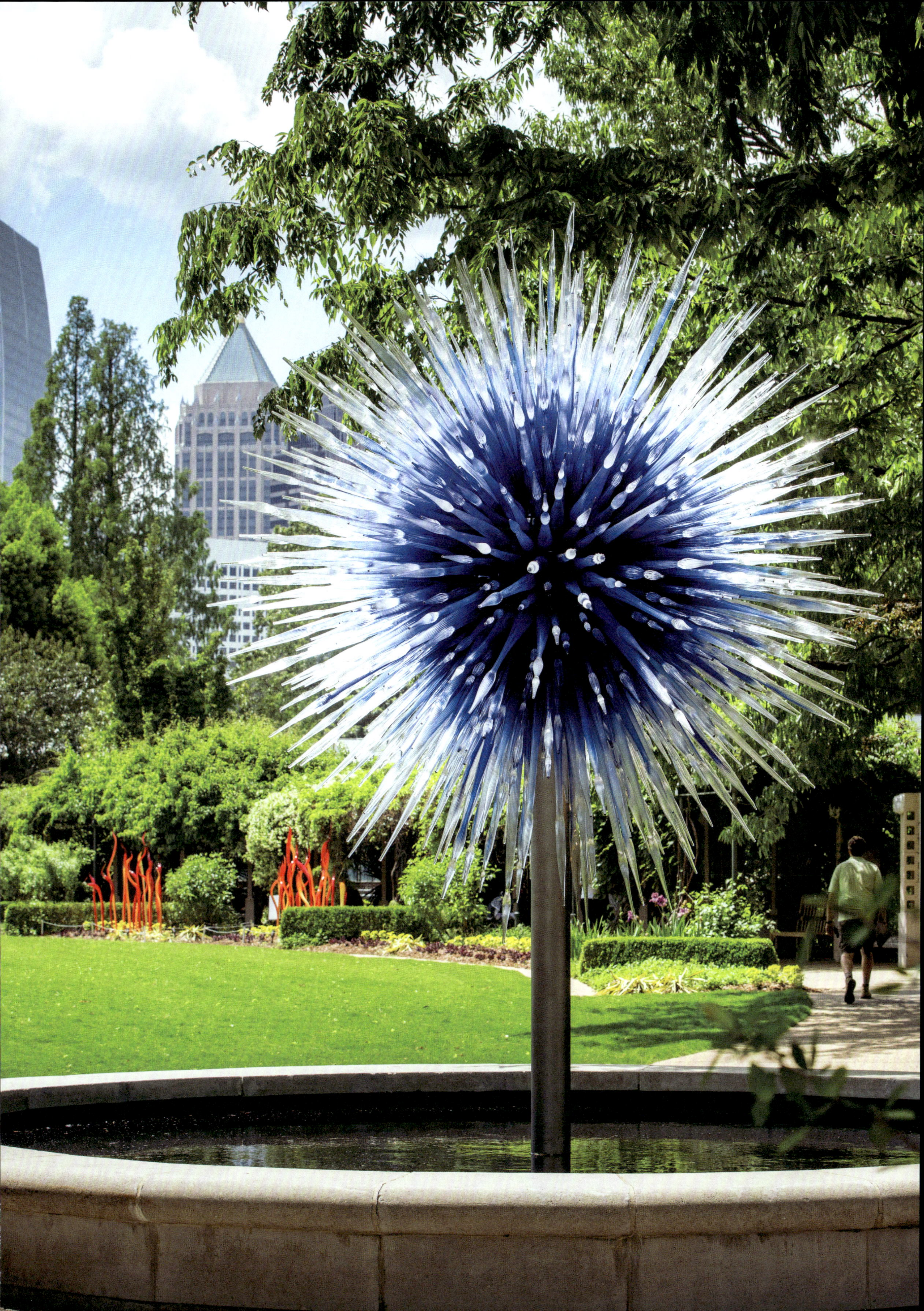

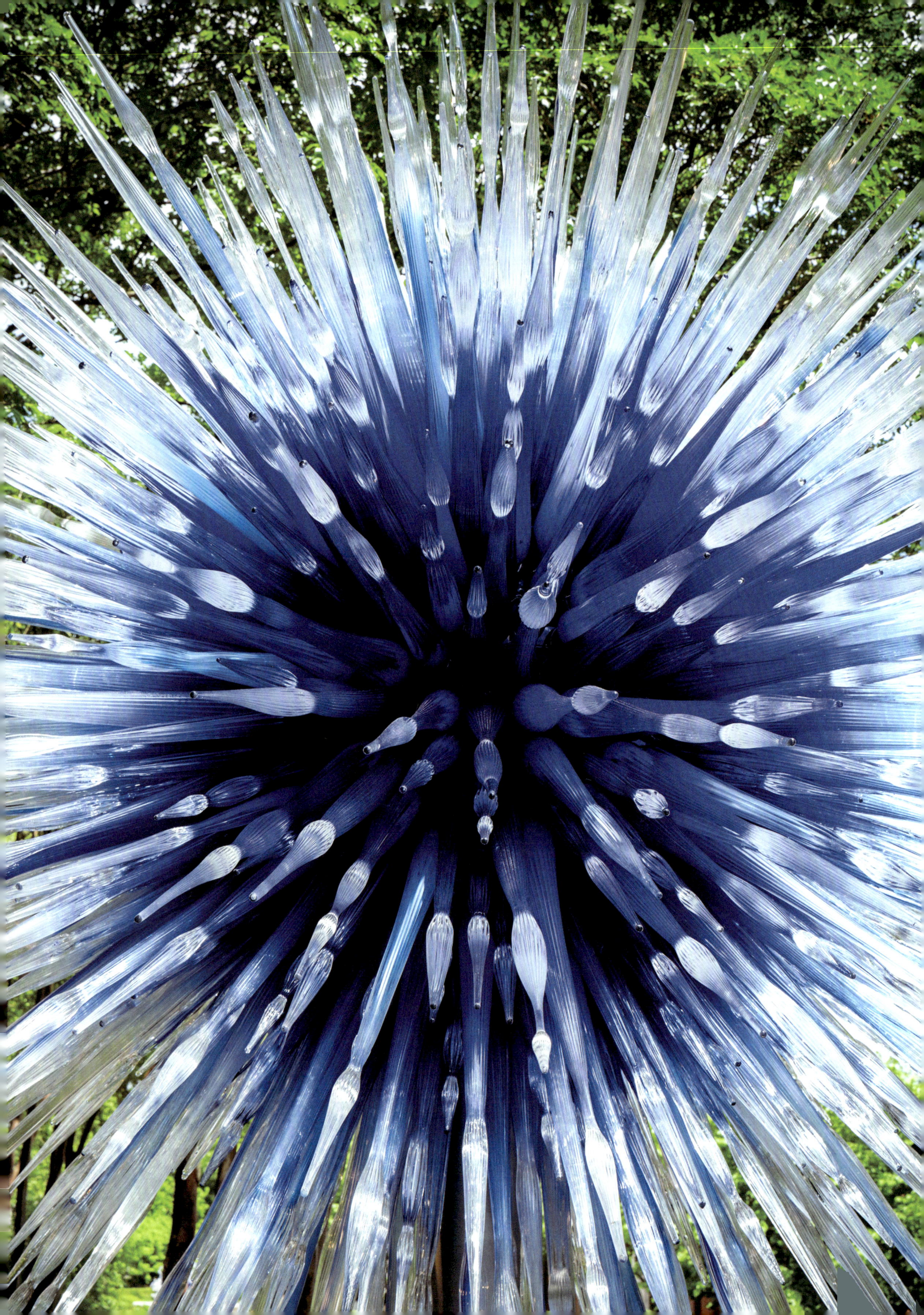

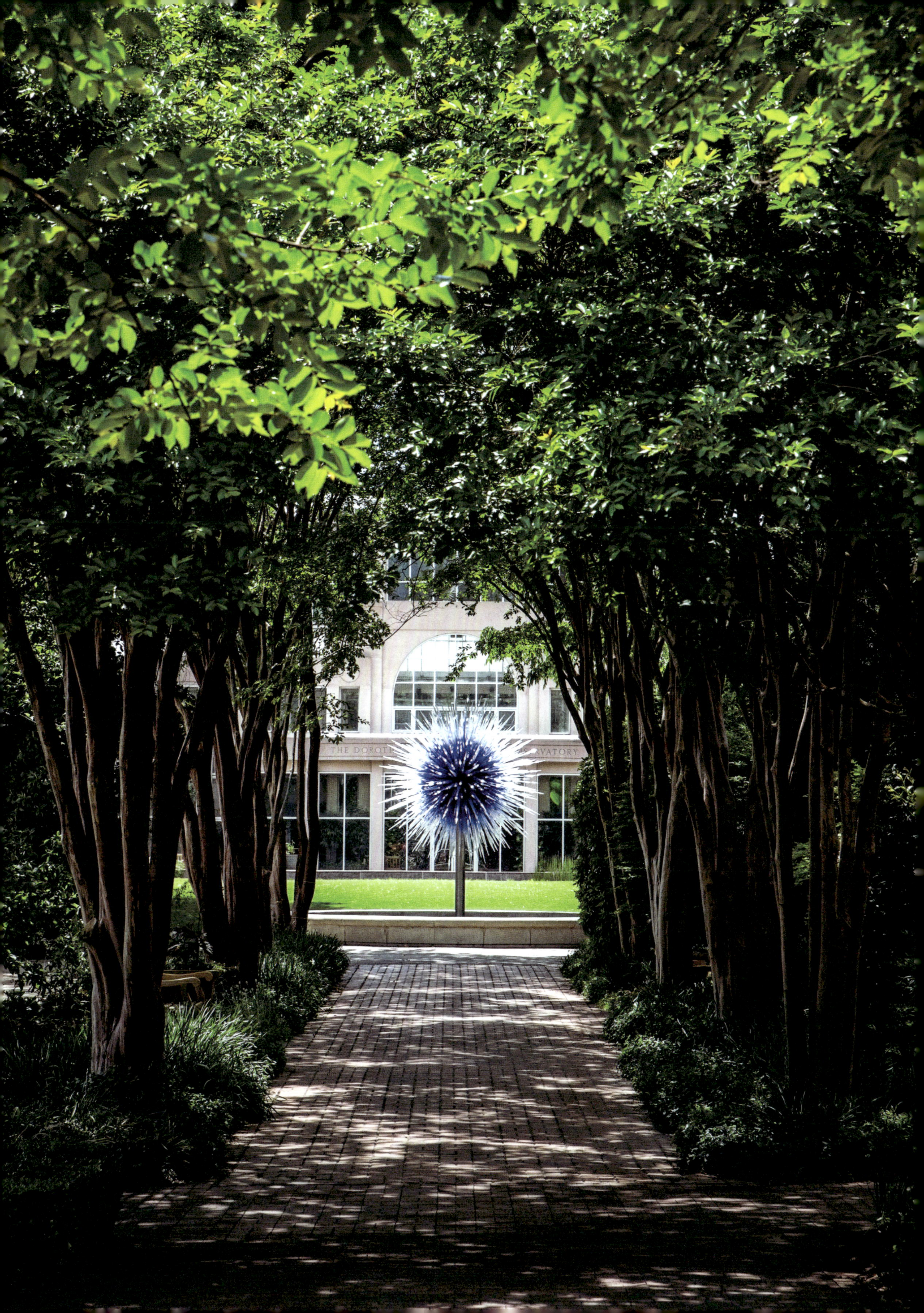

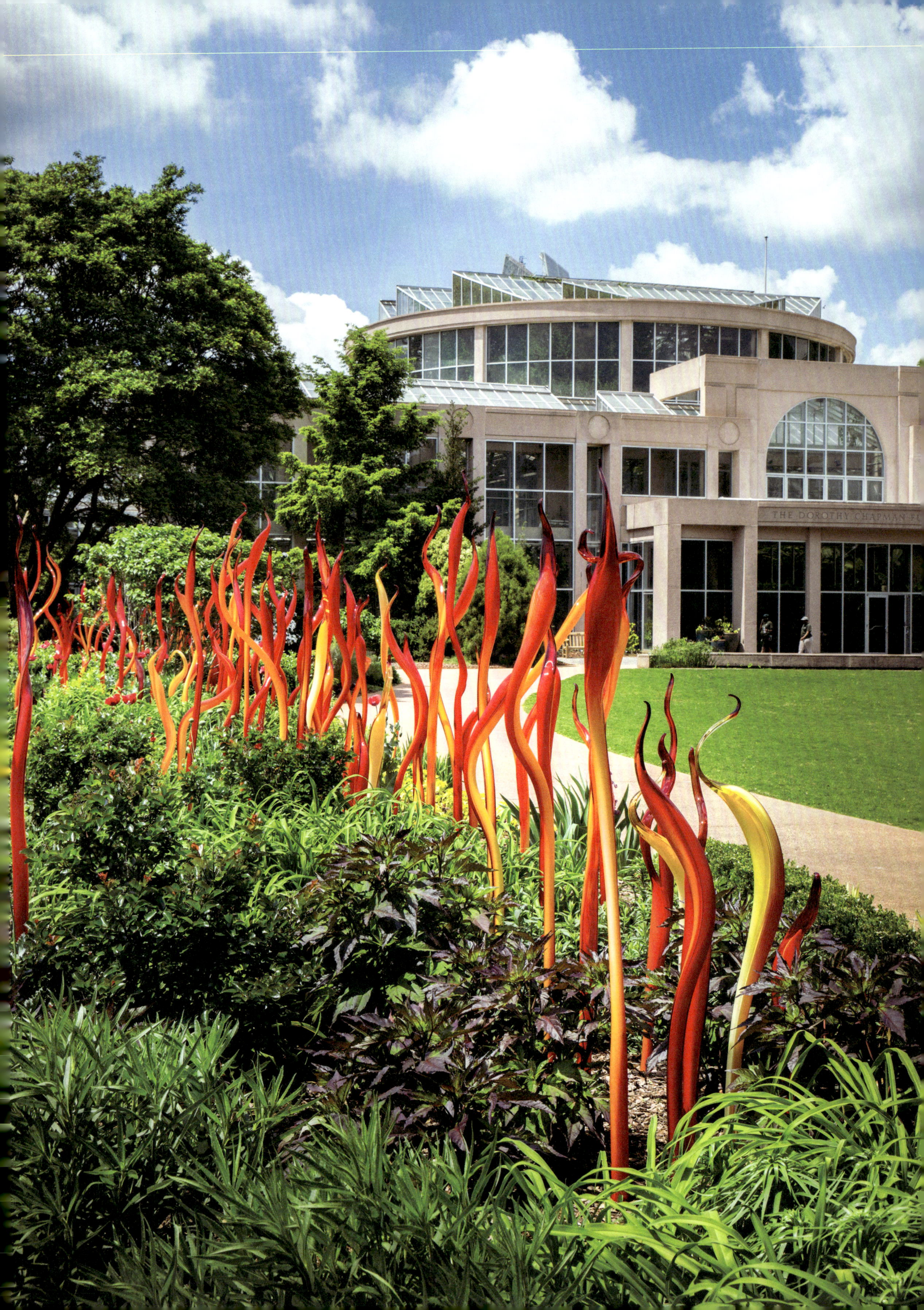
THE DOROTHY CHAPMAN

*Opposite and next*
**CARMEL AND RED FIORI**
2015, installed 2016

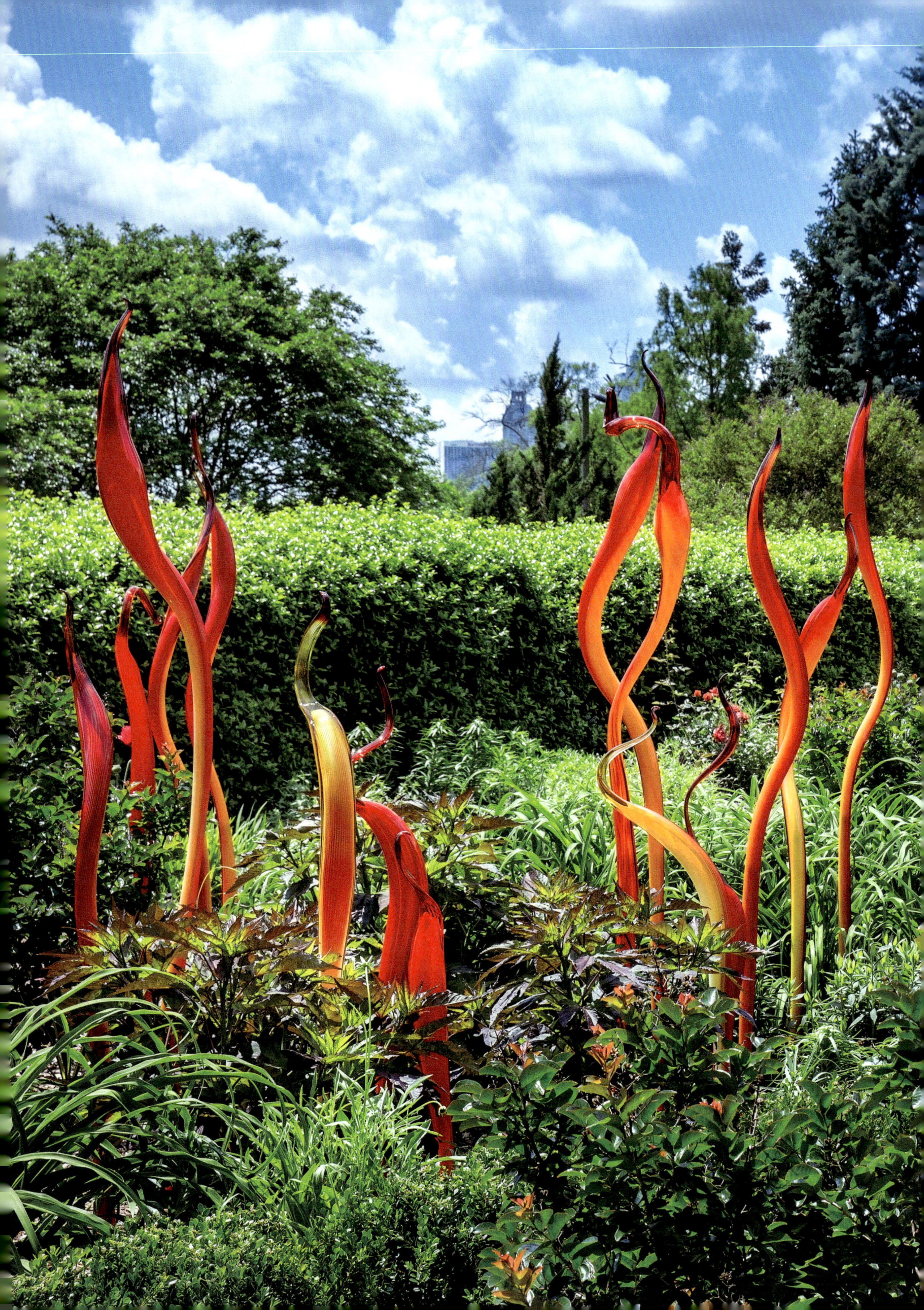

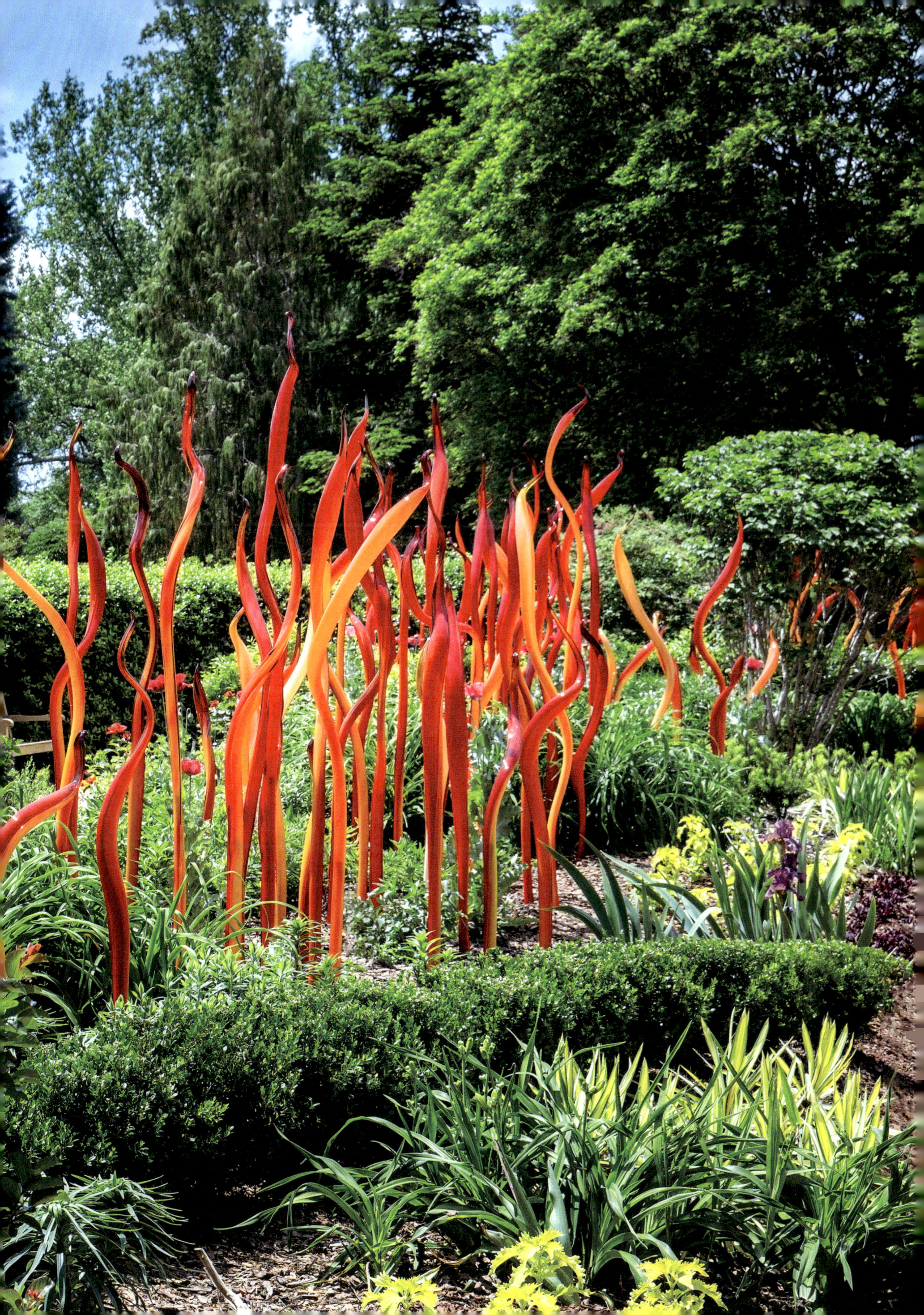

*Opposite*
**IMPERIAL BLUE IKEBANA WITH GREEN FROG FOOT STEMS**
2002, 56 x 37 x 13"
installed 2016

*Next*
**RUBY WINE IKEBANA WITH SUNLIGHT STEM**
2002, 63 x 19 x 20"
installed 2016

**RUSSET YELLOW PAINTBRUSH IKEBANA**
2006, 72 x 27 x 18"
installed 2016

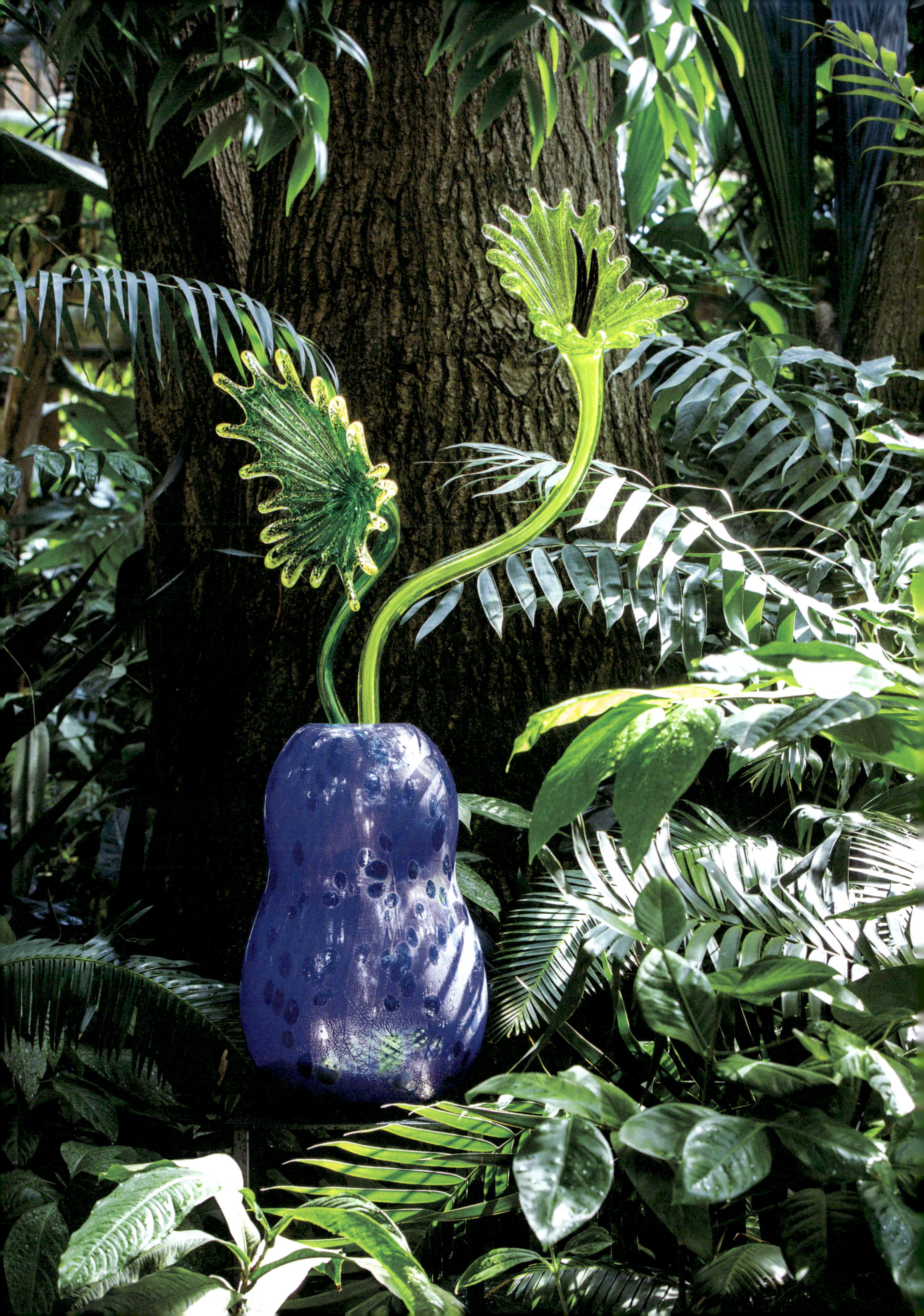

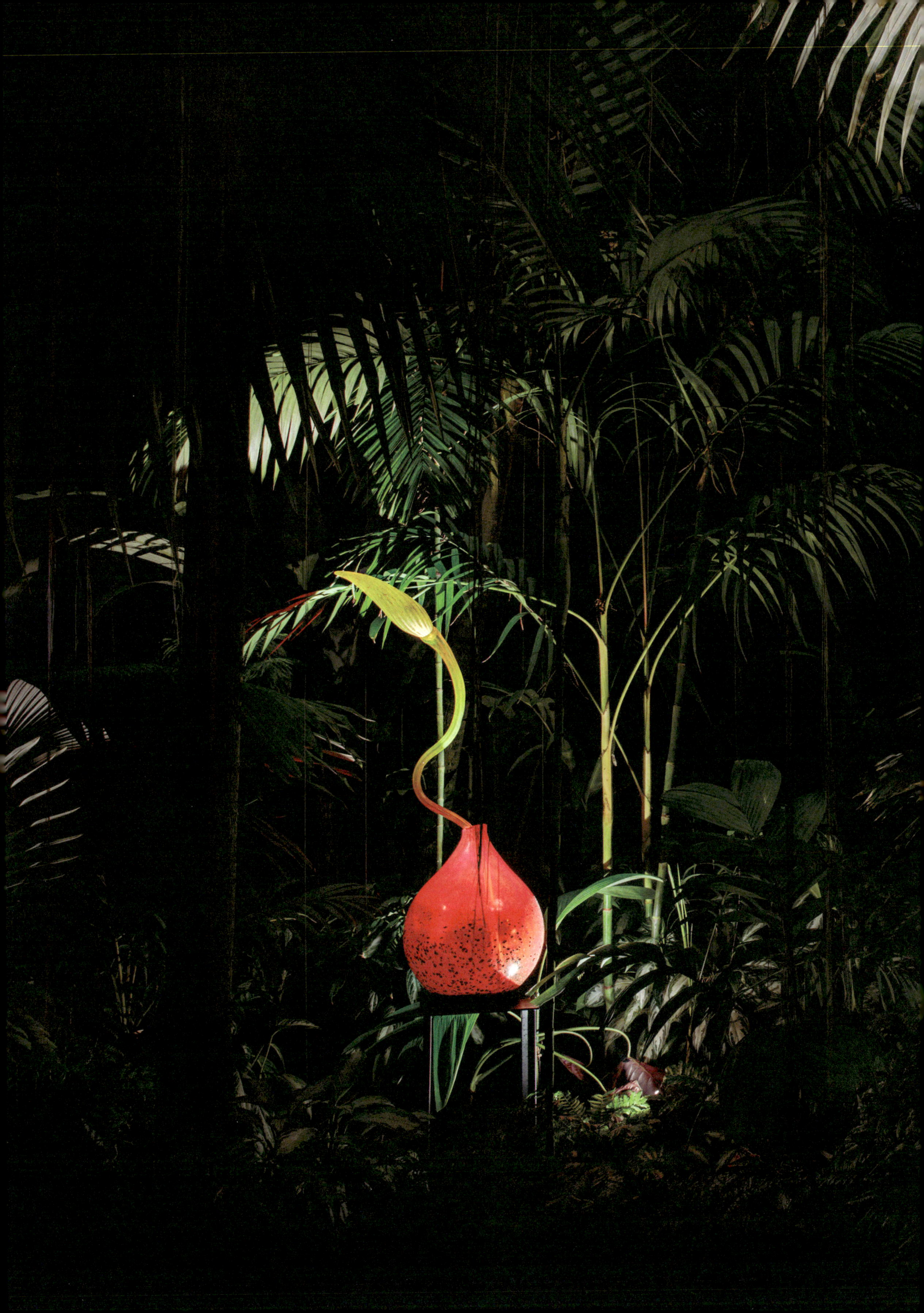

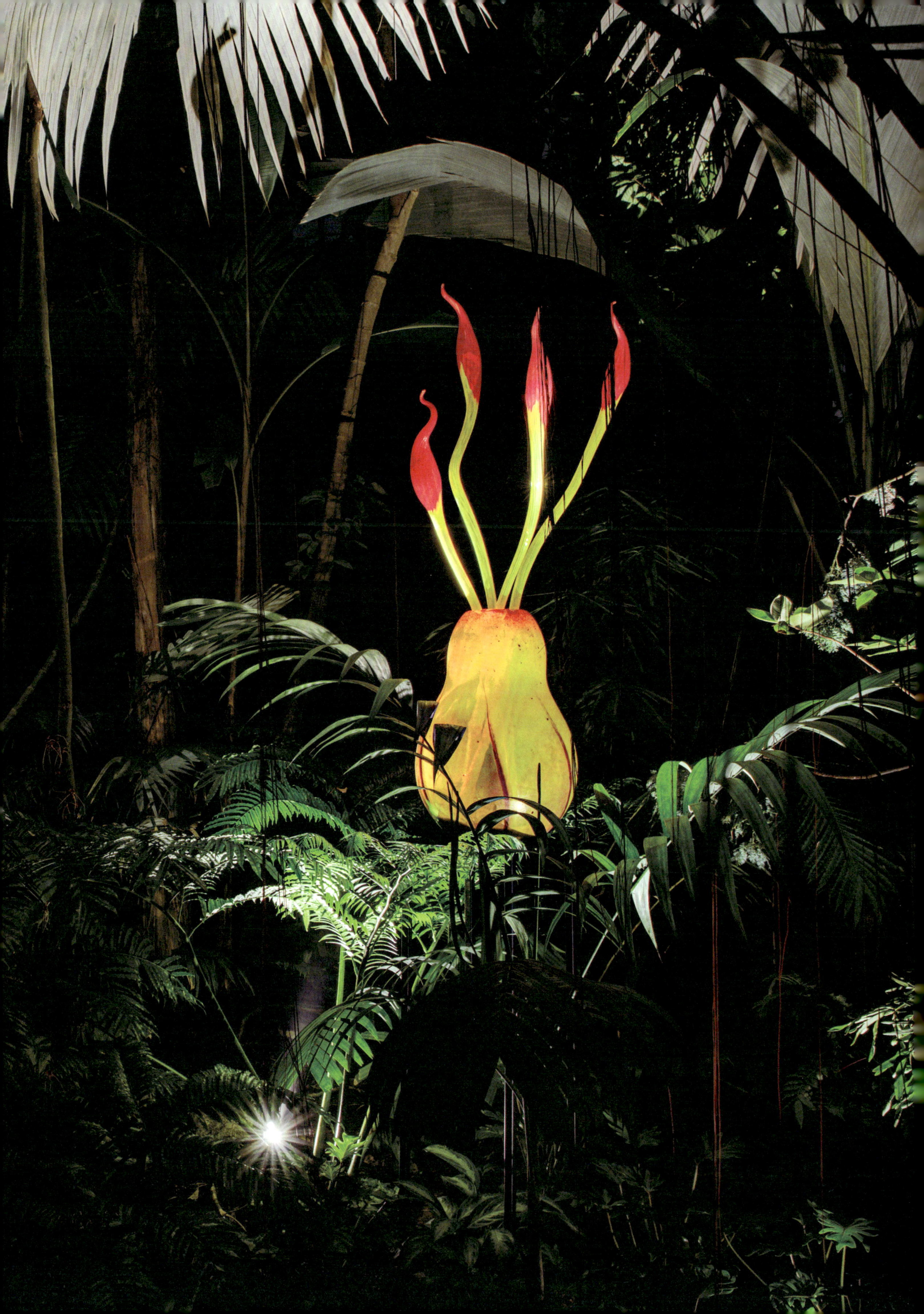

*Next (detail opposite)*

**SAPPHIRE NEON WITH NEODYMIUM REEDS, FLOATS, AND LOGS**

2015, 6 x 9 x 8'
installed 2016

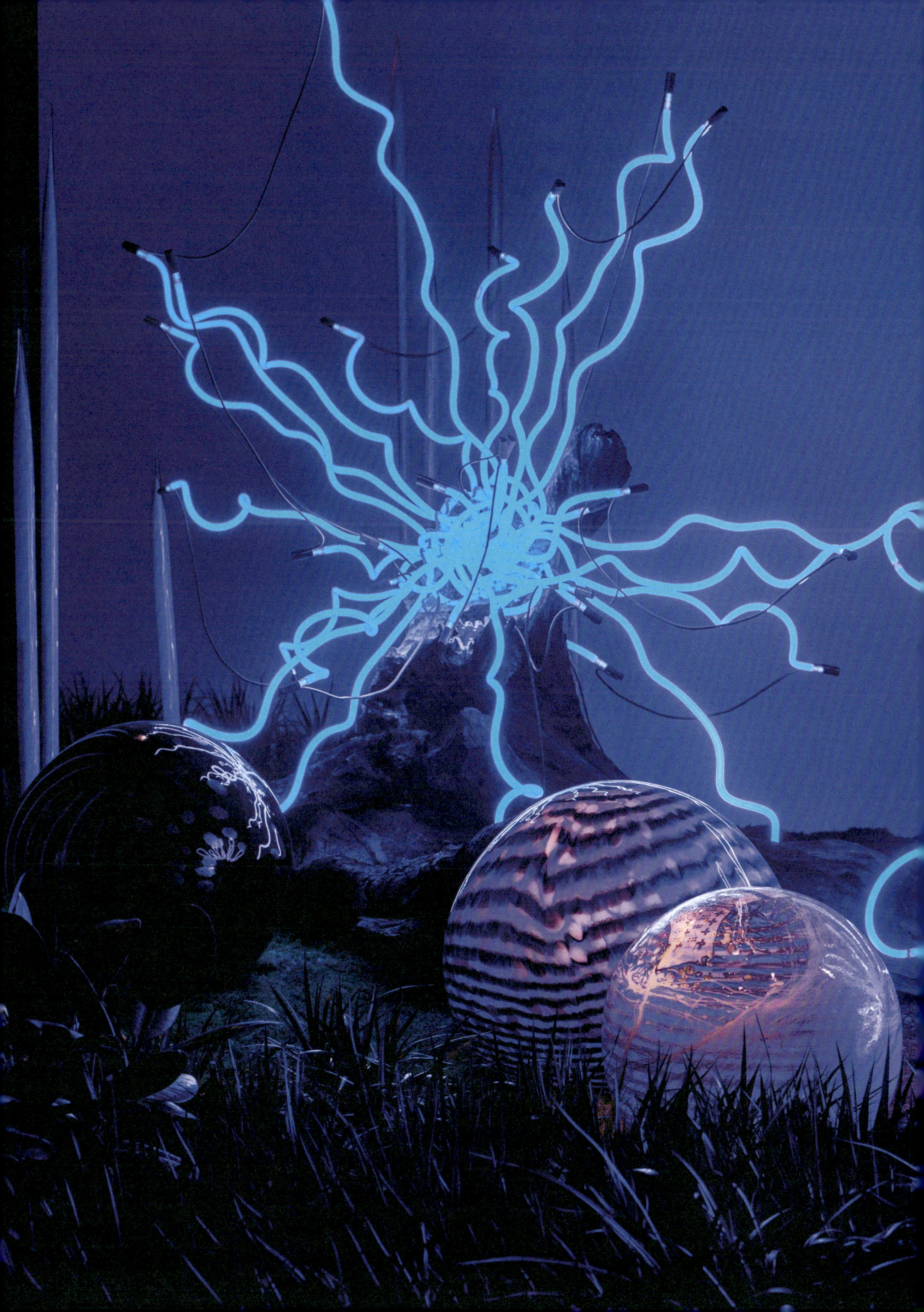

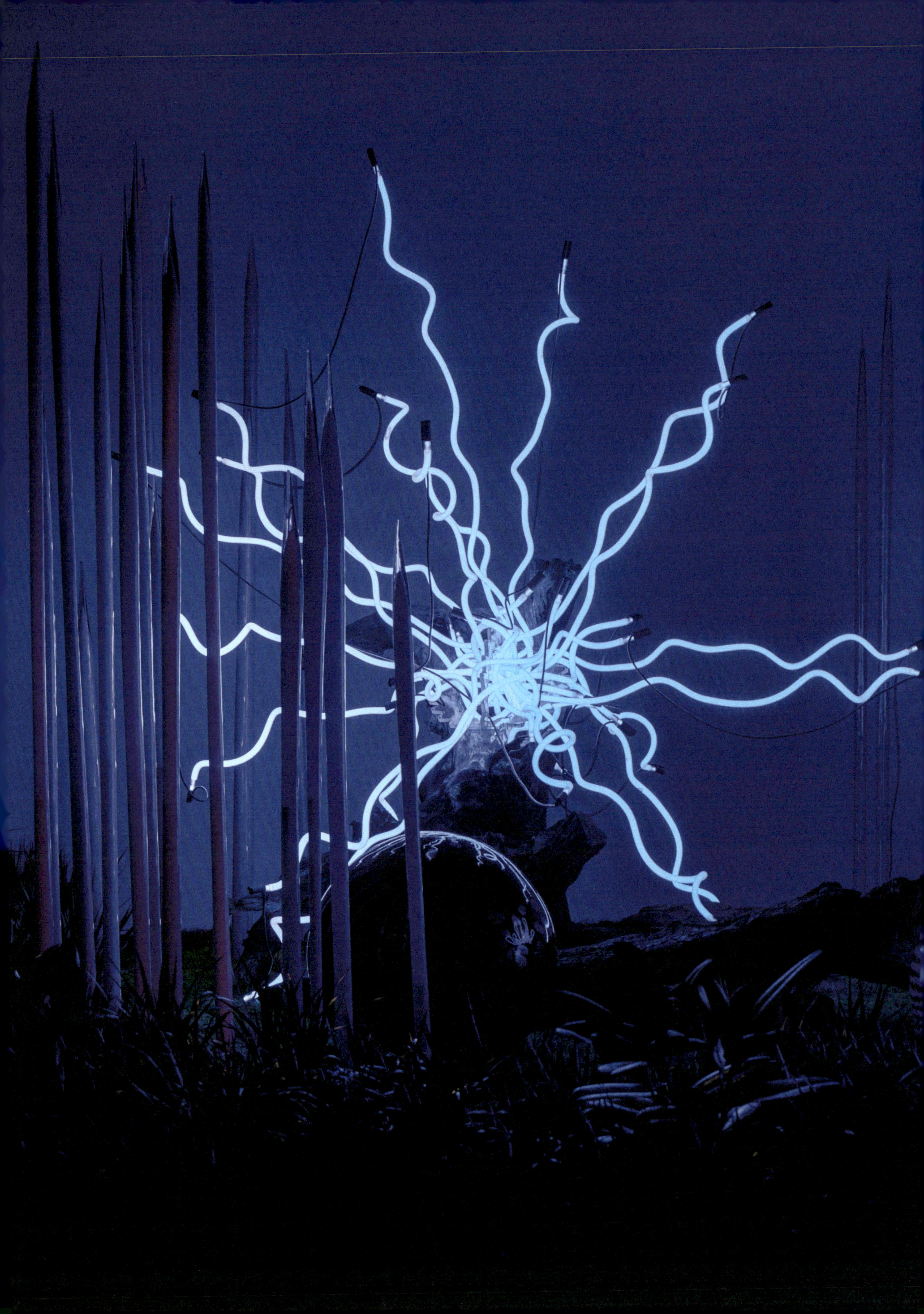

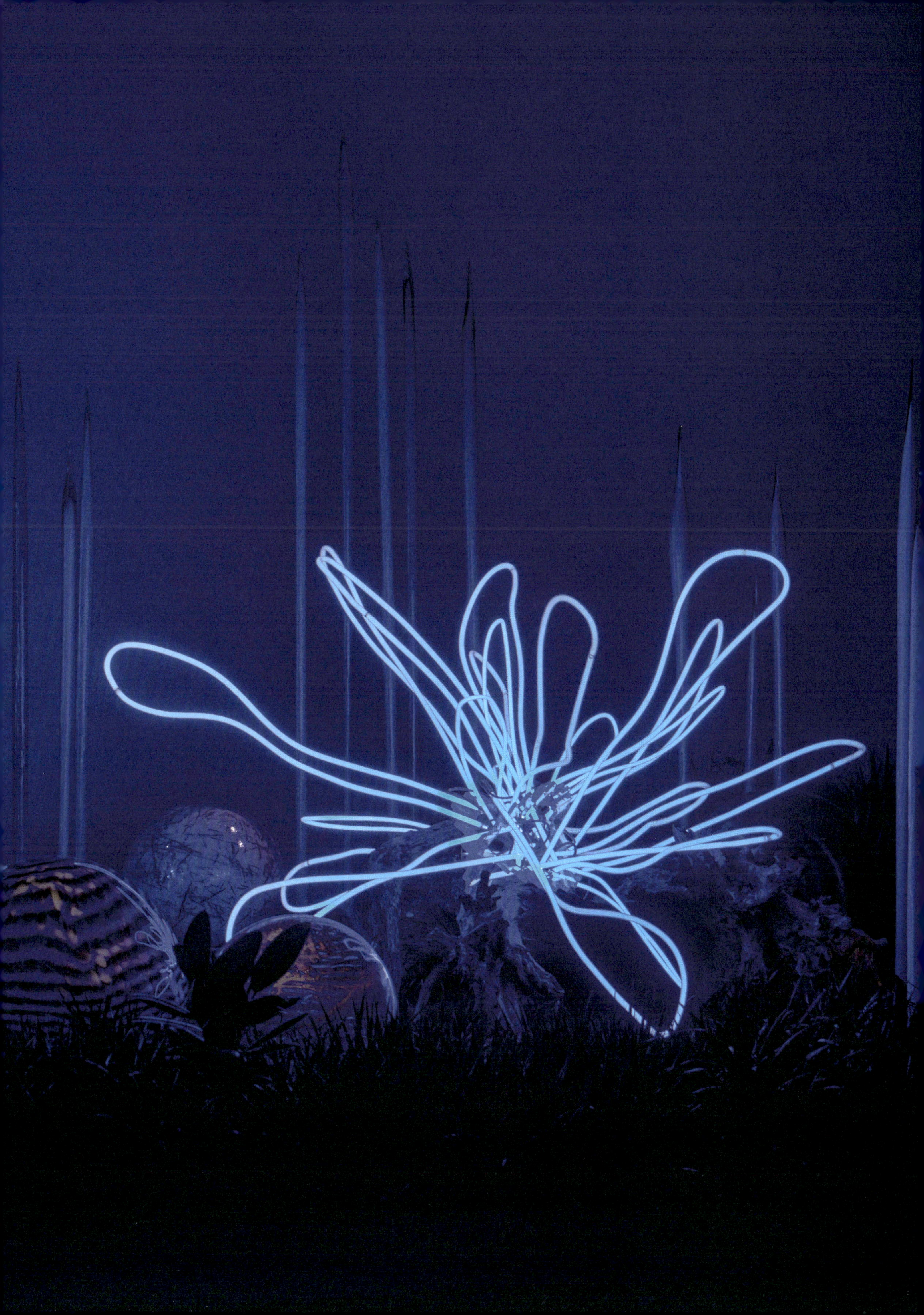

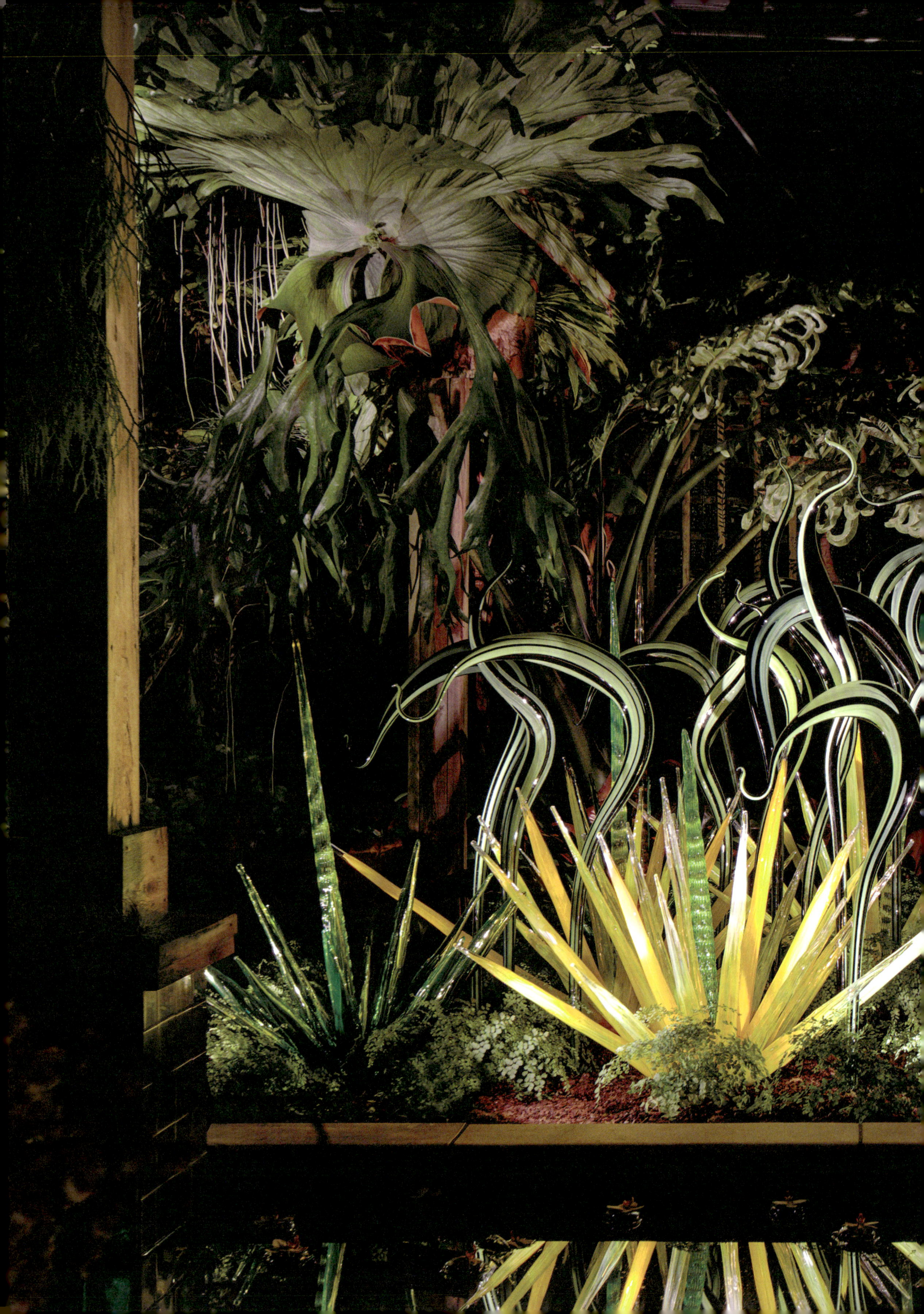

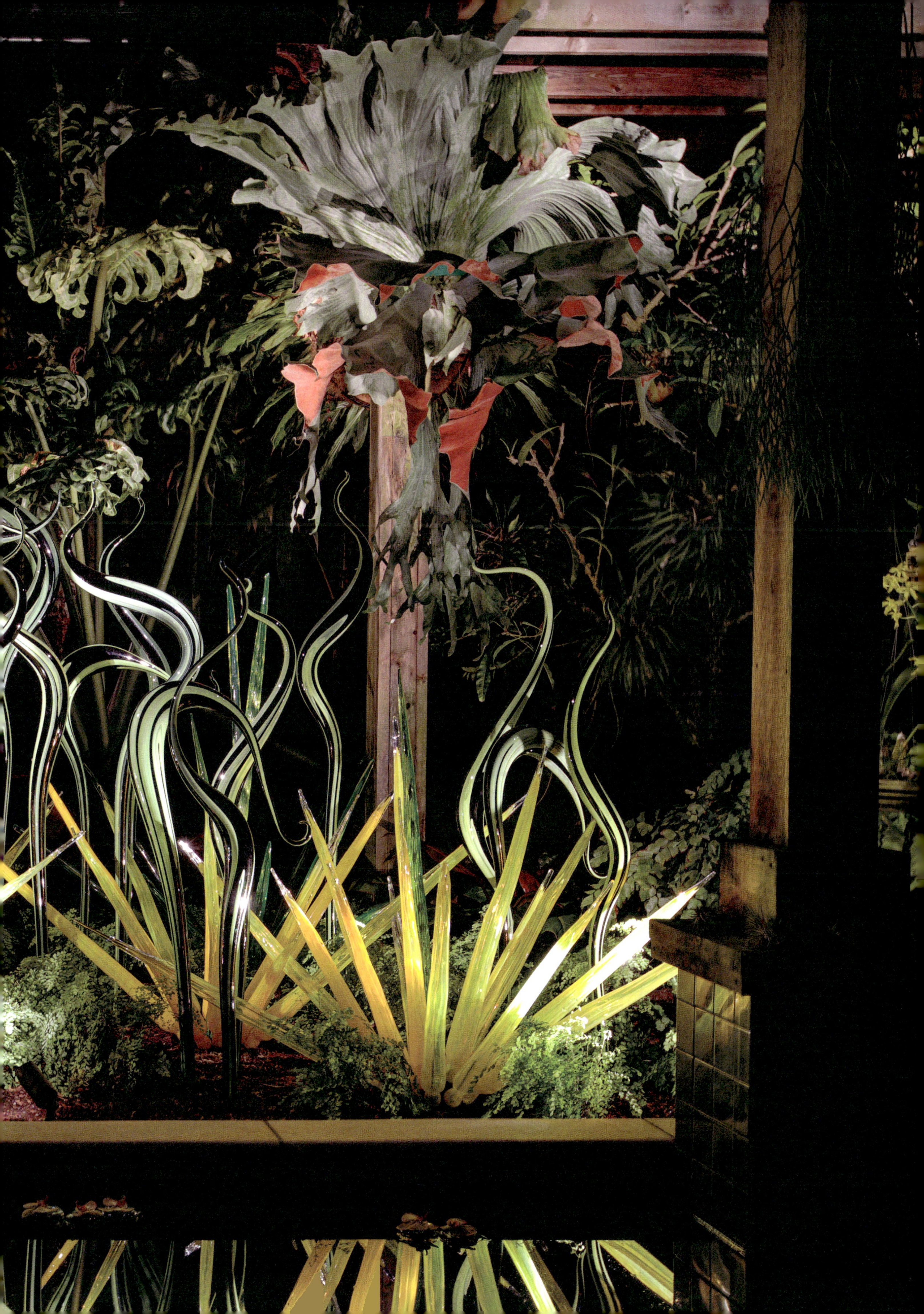

*Previous and next (detail opposite)*

**BLACK AND GREEN STRIPED HERONS WITH ICICLE CLUSTERS**

2015, 6 x 12½ x 17½'
installed 2016

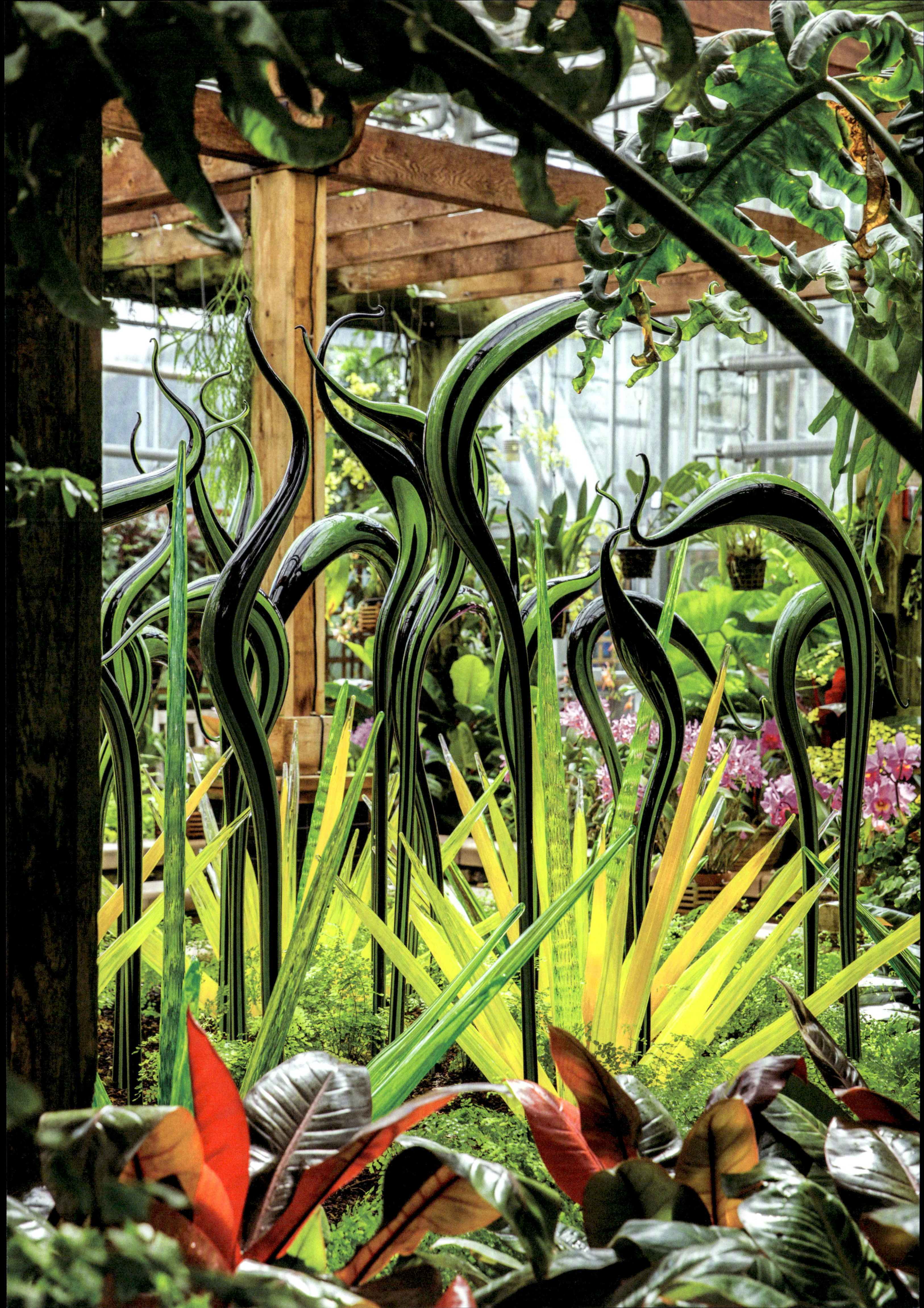

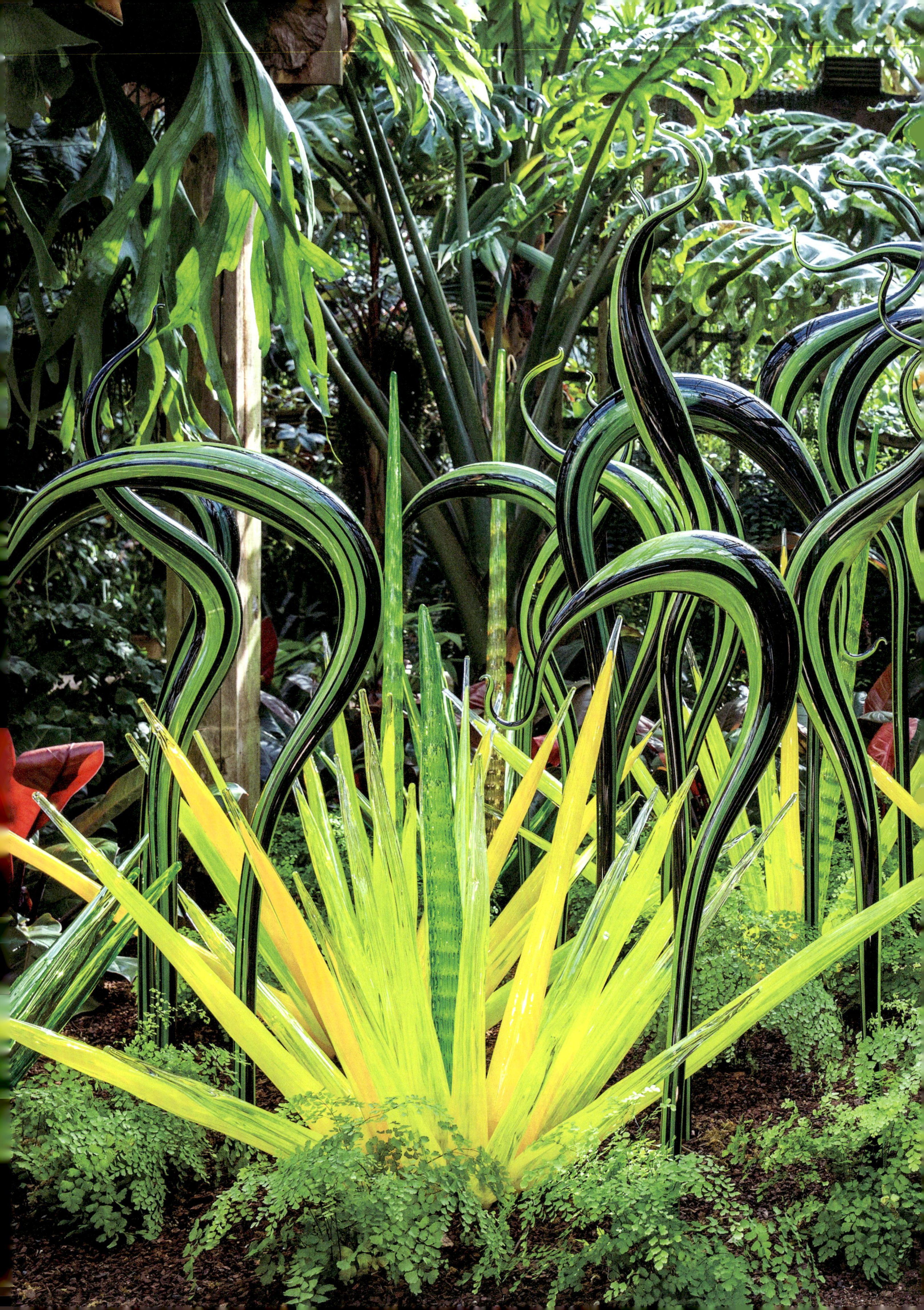

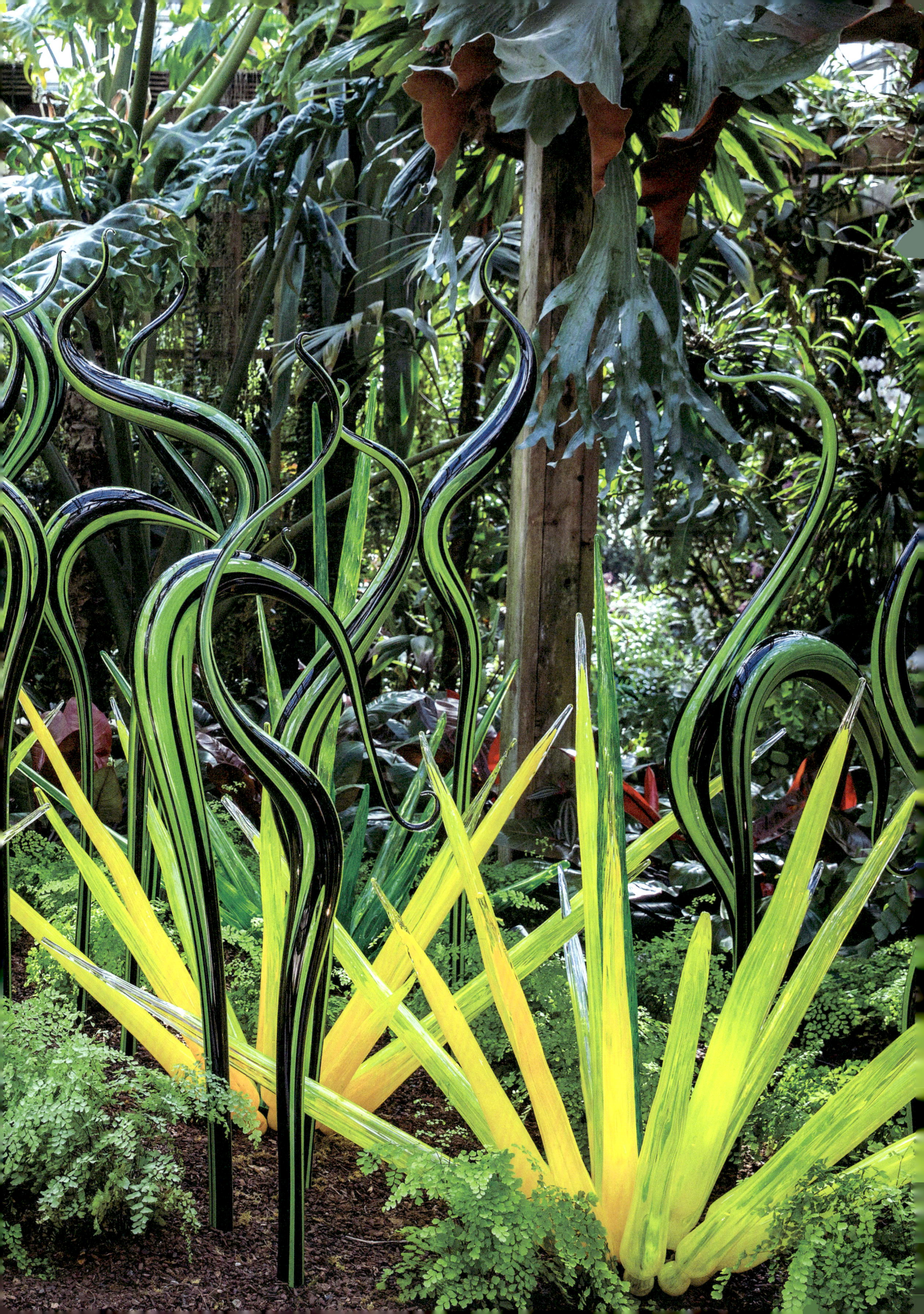

*Next (detail opposite)*
**ZEBRA REEDS**
2015, installed 2016

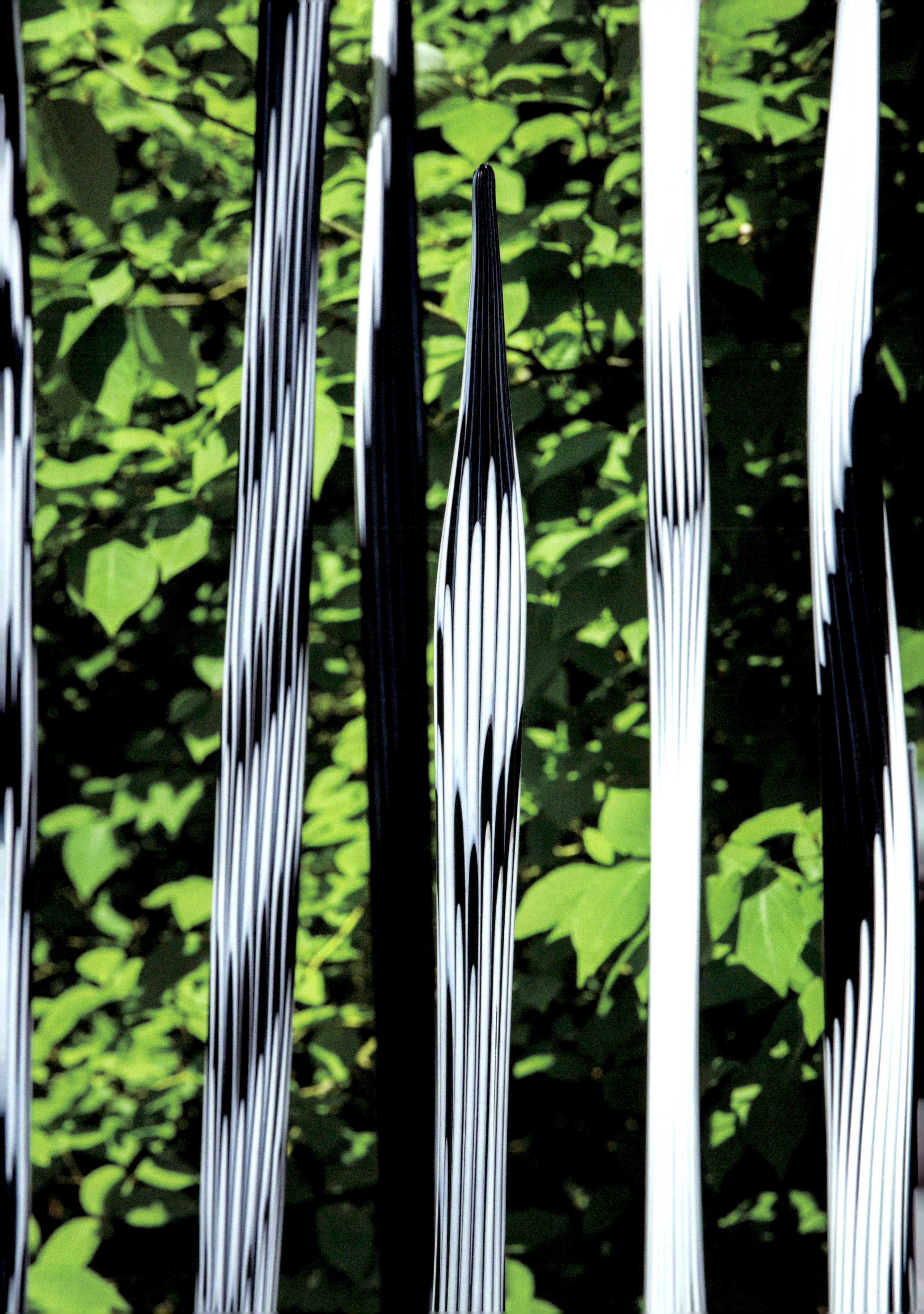

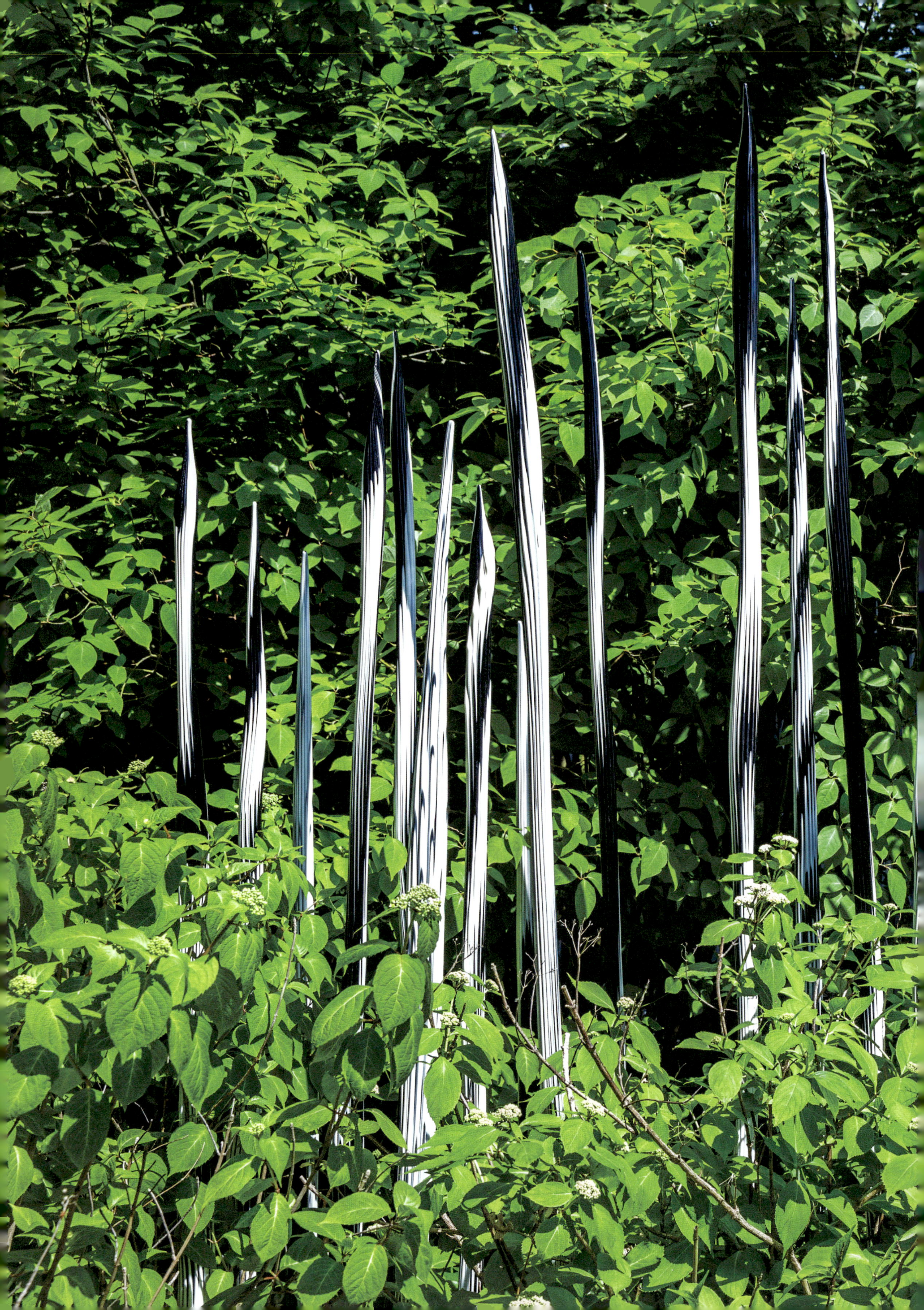

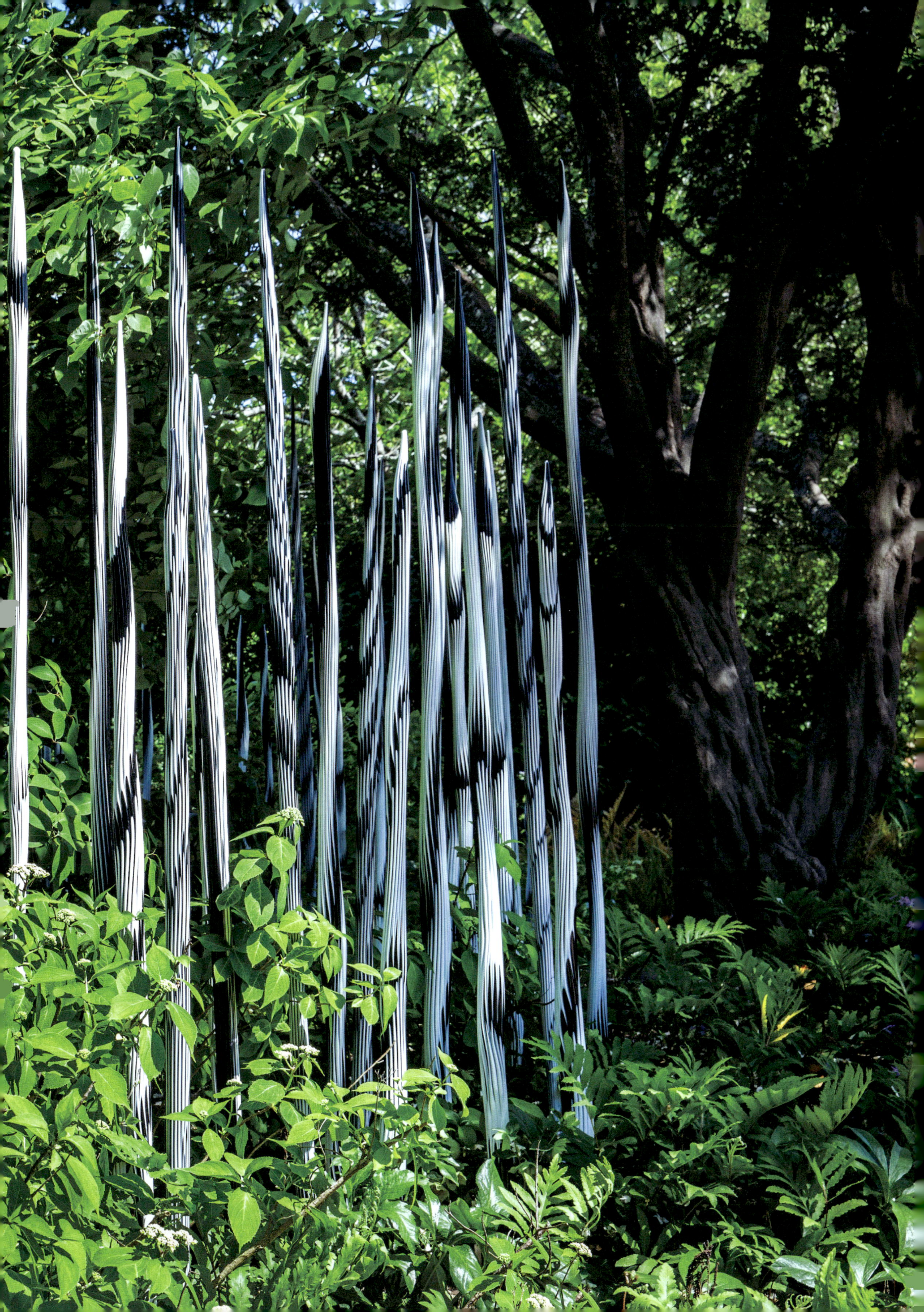

DALE CHIHULY

# CHRONOLOGY

# 1941–1967

1941

## Born September 20 in Tacoma, Washington, to George Chihuly and Viola Magnuson Chihuly.

Dale and Viola Chihuly, Tacoma, Washington, circa 1943

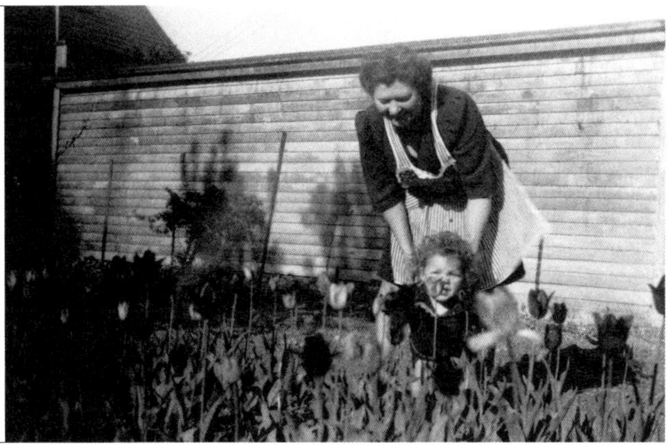

**1957** Older brother and only sibling, George, dies in a navy flight-training accident in Pensacola, Florida.

**1958** His father suffers a fatal heart attack at age fifty-one, and his mother has to go to work.

**1959** Graduates from high school in Tacoma. Enrolls at College of Puget Sound (now University of Puget Sound) in his hometown.

**1960** Transfers to University of Washington in Seattle, where he studies interior design and architecture.

**1961** Joins Delta Kappa Epsilon fraternity and becomes rush chairman. Learns to melt and fuse glass.

**1962** Interrupts his studies and travels to Florence to focus on art. Frustrated by his inability to speak Italian, he moves on to the Middle East.

**1963** Works on a kibbutz in Negev desert, Israel. Reinspired, returns to University of Washington and studies under Hope Foote and Warren Hill. In a weaving class with Doris Brockway, incorporates glass shards into woven tapestries.

**1964** Returns to Europe, visiting Leningrad and making the first of many trips to Ireland.

**1965** Receives BA in interior design from University of Washington. In his basement studio, blows his first glass bubble by melting stained glass and using a metal pipe.

**1966** Earns money for graduate school as a commercial fisherman in Alaska. Enters University of Wisconsin at Madison on a full scholarship, to study glassblowing in the first glass program in the United States, taught by Harvey Littleton.

**1967** After receiving MS in sculpture from University of Wisconsin, enrolls at Rhode Island School of Design (RISD) in Providence, where he begins exploration of environmental works using neon, argon, and blown glass. Awarded a Louis Comfort Tiffany Foundation Grant for work in glass. Artist Italo Scanga lectures at RISD, and the two start a lifelong friendship.

# 1968–1985

**1968** Receives MFA from RISD. Spends the first of four consecutive summers teaching at Haystack Mountain School of Crafts in Deer Isle, Maine. A Fulbright Fellowship awarded earlier in the year enables him to work and study in Europe. Becomes the first American glassblower to work in the prestigious Venini factory, on the island of Murano.

**1969** Makes pilgrimages to meet glass masters Erwin Eisch in Germany and Stanislav Libenský and his wife, Jaroslava Brychtová, in Czechoslovakia. Establishes the glass program at RISD, where he teaches for the next eleven years.

**1970** Meets James Carpenter, a student in RISD Illustration Department, and they begin a four-year collaboration.

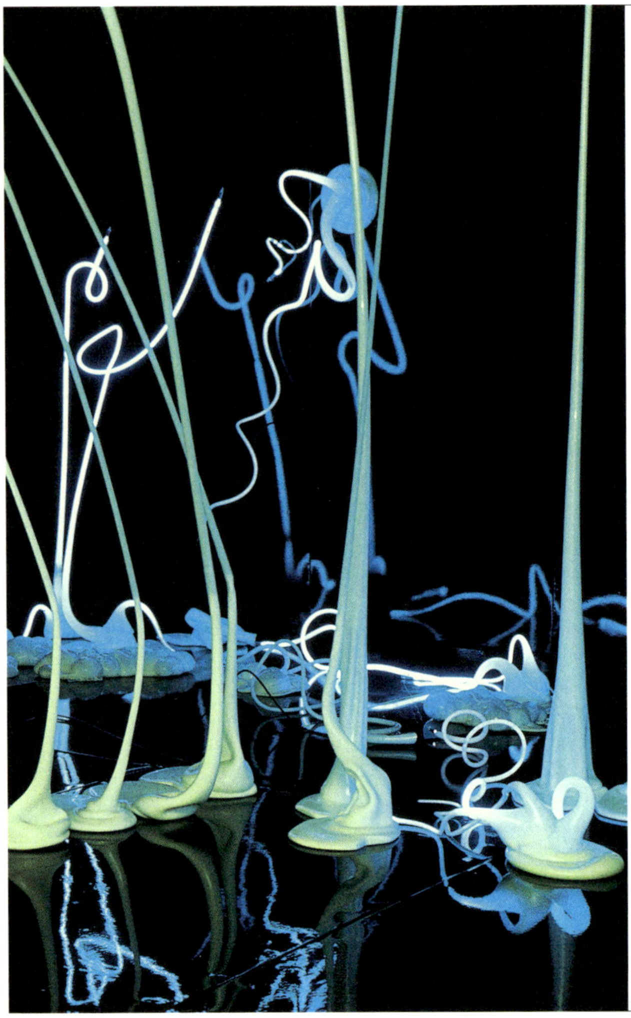

**1971**

On the site of a tree farm north of Seattle owned by art patrons Anne Gould Hauberg and John Hauberg, the Pilchuck Glass School experiment is started. *Pilchuck Pond*, Chihuly's first environmental installation at the school, is created that summer. In the fall, at RISD, he makes *20,000 Pounds of Ice and Neon*, *Glass Forest #1*, and *Glass Forest #2* with James Carpenter, installations that prefigure later environmental works by Chihuly.

*Glass Forest #1* (detail), 1971
Museum of Contemporary Crafts, New York City
Created in collaboration with James Carpenter

**1972** Collaborates with James Carpenter on more large-scale architectural projects. They create *Rondel Door* and *Cast Glass Door* at Pilchuck. In Providence, they have a conceptual breakthrough with *Dry Ice, Bent Glass and Neon.*

**1974** Works with James Carpenter and a group of students at Pilchuck to develop a technique for picking up glass thread drawings and incorporating them into larger glass pieces.

**1975** At RISD, begins *Navajo Blanket Cylinder* series. Kate Elliott and, later, Flora C. Mace fabricate the complex thread drawings for his artwork. He receives the first of two National Endowment for the Arts Visual Artists' Fellowships. Becomes artist-in-residence with Seaver Leslie at Artpark, an annual arts program on the Niagara Gorge in New York State. Begins *Irish Cylinders* and *Ulysses Cylinders* with Leslie and Mace.

**1976** An automobile accident in England leaves him, after weeks in the hospital and 256 stitches in his face, without sight in his left eye and with permanent damage to his right ankle and foot. After recuperating, he returns to Providence to serve as head of the Department of Sculpture and the Program in Glass at RISD. Henry Geldzahler, curator of contemporary art at the Metropolitan Museum of Art in New York, acquires three *Navajo Blanket Cylinders* for the museum's collection—a turning point in Chihuly's career and the start of the artist's friendship with both the curator and the museum director then, Thomas Hoving.

**1977** His *Basket* series—inspired by Northwest Coast Indian baskets he sees at Washington State History Museum in Tacoma—is first made at Pilchuck with Benjamin Moore as gaffer and exhibited at Seattle Art Museum. Continues teaching at both RISD and Pilchuck.

**1978** Meets Pilchuck student William Morris, and the two begin a close, eight-year working relationship. A solo show at the Renwick Gallery, Smithsonian Institution, in Washington, D.C., is another career milestone.

**1979** Dislocates his shoulder in a bodysurfing accident and relinquishes the gaffer position for good. William Morris becomes his chief gaffer for several years. Chihuly begins to make drawings as a way to communicate his designs.

**1980** Resigns his teaching position at RISD but returns periodically in the 1980s as artist-in-residence. Begins *Seaform* series. Creates his first architectural commission: windows for Shaare Emeth Synagogue in St. Louis.

**1981** Begins *Macchia* series.

**1982** First catalog is published: *Chihuly Glass*, designed by RISD colleague and friend Malcolm Grear.

**1983** Returns to Pacific Northwest after sixteen years on the East Coast.

**1984** Begins work on *Soft Cylinder* series, with Flora C. Mace and Joey Kirkpatrick executing the glass drawings. Honored as RISD President's Fellow at the Whitney Museum in New York.

**1985** Purchases the Buffalo Shoe Company Building just east of Lake Union in Seattle and begins

# 1986–2001

restoring it for use as a primary studio and residence.

**1986** Begins *Persian* series with Martin Blank as gaffer, assisted by Robbie Miller. Establishes his first hotshop in Van de Kamp Building near Lake Union in Seattle. *Dale Chihuly Objets de Verre* opens at Musée des Arts Décoratifs, Palais du Louvre, in Paris.

**1987** Donates permanent collection to Tacoma Art Museum in memory of his brother and father (adding works to the collection years later in memory of his mother). Marries playwright Sylvia Peto.

**1988** Inspired by Italian Art Deco glass, begins *Venetian* series with Italian glass master Lino Tagliapietra, working from Chihuly's drawings; Benjamin Moore also plays a very important role, including translator.

**1989** With Lino Tagliapietra and fellow glass master Pino Signoretto, as well as a team of glassblowers, begins *Putti* series at Pilchuck. With Tagliapietra, Chihuly creates *Ikebana* series, inspired by travels to Japan and exposure to ikebana masters.

**1990** Purchases historic Pocock Building located on Lake Union, realizing his dream of being on the water in Seattle. Renovated and renamed the Boathouse, it serves as studio and hotshop. Returns to Japan.

**1991** Begins *Niijima Float* series with Richard Royal as gaffer, creating some of the largest pieces of glass ever blown by hand. Chihuly and Sylvia Peto divorce.

**1992** Begins *Chandelier* series with a hanging sculpture at Seattle Art Museum. Designs sets for Seattle Opera's 1993 production of Debussy's *Pelléas et Mélisande*.

**1993** With Lino Tagliapietra, begins *Piccolo Venetian* series. Creates *100,000 Pounds of Ice and Neon*, a temporary installation in Tacoma Dome.

**1994** Creates five installations for Tacoma's Union Station Federal Courthouse. Supports Hilltop Artists, a glassblowing program in Tacoma for at-risk youths, created by friend Kathy Kaperick. Within two years, the program partners with Tacoma Public School District.

**1995** An international project, *Chihuly Over Venice*, begins with a glassblowing session in Nuutajärvi, Finland, and subsequent blow at Waterford Crystal factory, Ireland.

**1996** After a blow in Monterrey, Mexico, *Chihuly Over Venice* culminates with the installation of fourteen *Chandeliers* around Venice and a glassblowing session with Pino Signoretto and Lino Tagliapietra on Murano. Creates his first permanent outdoor installation, *Icicle Creek Chandelier*, for Sleeping Lady resort in Leavenworth, Washington.

**1997** Expands series of experimental plastics he calls Polyvitro. Travels to Japan to blow glass at Niijima Glass Art Center and creates several temporary outdoor *Float* installations. Travels with his team to a glass factory in Vianne, France, and they work with local glassblowers to create new works, some using industrial molds.

**1998** Participates in Sydney Arts Festival in Australia. A son, Jackson Viola Chihuly, is born February 12 to Dale Chihuly and Leslie Jackson. Creates architectural installations for Benaroya Hall, Seattle; Bellagio, Las Vegas; and Atlantis, Bahamas.

**1999** Begins *Jerusalem Cylinder* series with gaffer James Mongrain. Chihuly starts an ambitious exhibition, *Chihuly in the Light of Jerusalem 2000*, at Tower of David Museum of the History of Jerusalem. Just outside the museum, builds a sixty-foot-long wall made of twenty-four massive blocks of ice shipped from Alaska.

**2000** Creates *La Tour de Lumière* sculpture as part of *Contemporary American Sculpture* exhibition in Monte Carlo. More than one million visitors enter Tower of David Museum to see *Chihuly in the Light of Jerusalem 2000*, breaking the world attendance record for a temporary exhibition during 1999–2000.

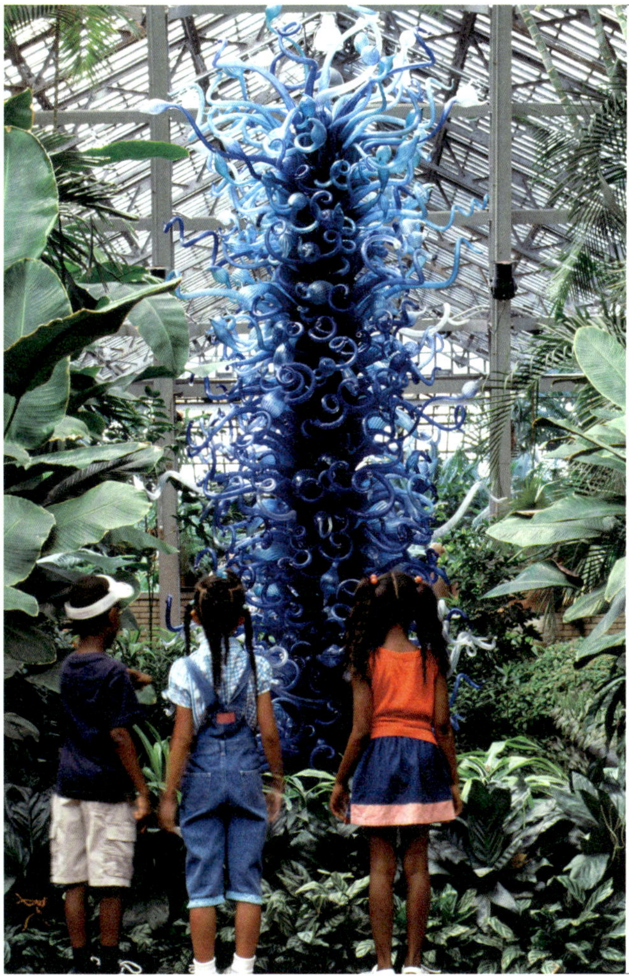

**2001**

*Chihuly at the V&A* opens at Victoria and Albert Museum, London. Artist Italo Scanga dies after more than three decades as friend and mentor. *Chihuly in the Park: A Garden of Glass*, at Garfield Park Conservatory, Chicago, begins *Garden Cycle*, a series of exhibitions in conservatories and gardens.

*Peacock Blue Tower*, 2001, 17 x 7'
Garfield Park Conservatory, Chicago

# 2002–2016

**2002** Creates large-scale installations for Winter Olympic Games in Salt Lake City. Chihuly Bridge of Glass is dedicated in Tacoma; conceived by Chihuly and designed in collaboration with Arthur Andersson of Andersson•Wise Architects, it is a pedestrian overpass featuring three permanent installations of Chihuly's work.

**2003** Begins *Fiori* series with gaffer Joey DeCamp and creates first *Mille Fiori*, for exhibition at Tacoma Art Museum. A garden exhibition opens at Franklin Park Conservatory, Columbus, Ohio.

**2004**

## Orlando Museum of Art and Museum of Fine Arts, St. Petersburg, Florida, collaborate and present complementary exhibitions of his work. Installs garden exhibition at Atlanta Botanical Garden.

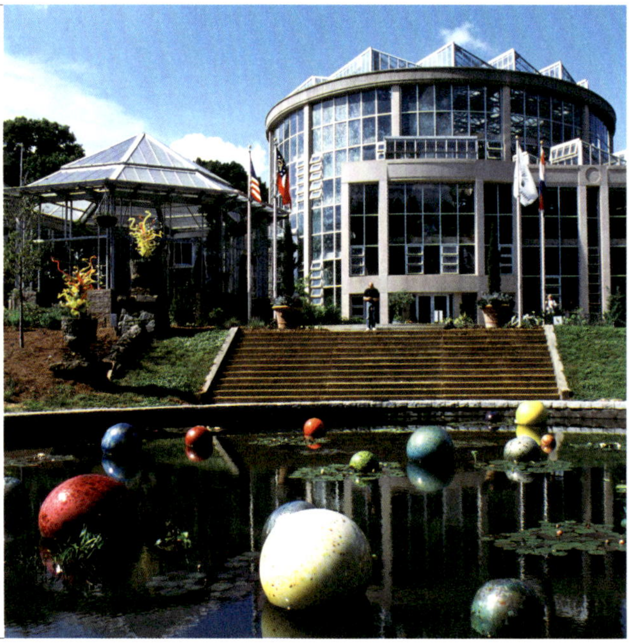

Dorothy Chapman Fuqua Conservatory
Atlanta Botanical Garden, 2004

**2005** Marries Leslie Jackson. Installs garden exhibition at Royal Botanic Gardens, Kew, outside London. Exhibits at Fairchild Tropical Botanic Garden, Coral Gables, Florida.

**2006** Mother, Viola, dies at age ninety-eight in Tacoma. Between April and June, begins *Black* series; exhibits at Missouri Botanical Garden, St. Louis; begins *Clear* series; and exhibits at New York Botanical Garden. *Chihuly in Tacoma*—a weeklong residency featuring hotshop sessions at Museum of Glass—reunites Chihuly and glassblowers from important periods of his career.

**2007** Exhibits at Phipps Conservatory and Botanical Gardens, Pittsburgh. Creates stage set for Seattle Symphony's production of Béla Bartók's opera, *Bluebeard's Castle*; the set will continue to be used in productions over the next several years, including Milwaukee, Nashville, and Buffalo, as well as Tel Aviv, Israel.

**2008** Presents exhibition at de Young Museum, San Francisco. Returns to his alma mater with an exhibition at RISD Museum of Art. Exhibits at Desert Botanical Garden in Phoenix.

**2009** Begins *Silvered* series. Participates in 53rd Venice Biennale with *Mille Fiori Venezia* installation. Returns to Franklin Park Conservatory, Columbus, Ohio, with a garden exhibition. Creates commission with multiple installations at island resort of Sentosa, Singapore.

**2010** Creates temporary installations outdoors at Kennedy Center for Performing Arts in Washington, D.C., and Salk Institute for Biological Studies in La Jolla, California. Presents exhibitions at Frederik Meijer Gardens & Sculpture Park in Grand Rapids, Michigan, and Cheekwood Botanical Garden and Museum of Art, Nashville. Begins *White* series.

**2011** Holds exhibitions at Museum of Fine Arts, Boston, and Tacoma Art Museum.

**2012** Exhibits at Dallas Arboretum and Botanical Garden. *Chihuly Garden and Glass* opens at Seattle Center; the long-term exhibition of the artist's work features gallery spaces, a sculpture garden, and a glasshouse designed by Chihuly. Exhibits at Virginia Museum of Fine Arts, Richmond.

**2013** Montreal Museum of Fine Arts holds exhibition of Chihuly art. Begins *Rotolo* series with gaffer James Mongrain. With Seaver Leslie, revisits the *Irish Cylinders* from nearly forty years ago with new *Ulysses Cylinders* inspired by the James Joyce novel.

**2014** At Clinton Presidential Library and Museum, Little Rock, Arkansas, displays temporary installations. Exhibition opens at Denver Botanic Gardens. Shows the new *Ulysses Cylinders* at Dublin Castle in Ireland.

**2015** An exhibition of Chihuly's drawings opens at Museum of Glass, Tacoma. The Toyama Glass Art Museum, in Toyama, Japan, commissions permanent installations of his work. Chihuly's set for the opera *Bluebeard's Castle* reappears in performances in Wichita, Kansas; and Norfolk, Virginia.

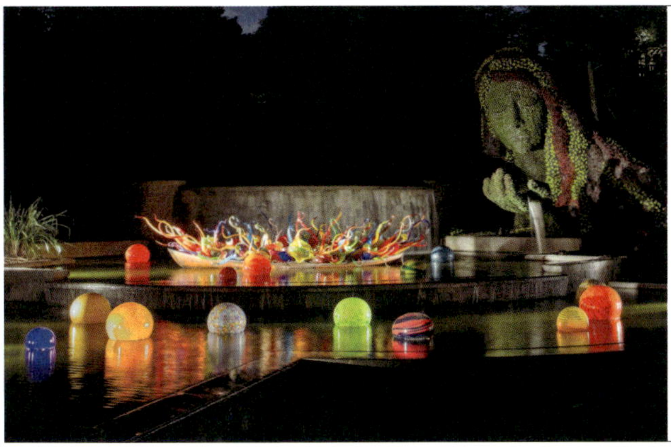

**2016**

## Returns to Atlanta Botanical Garden. Exhibits at Royal Ontario Museum, Toronto.

*Fiori Boat*, 2016, 4½ x 21 x 9½'
Atlanta Botanical Garden

DALE CHIHULY

# BIOGRAPHY

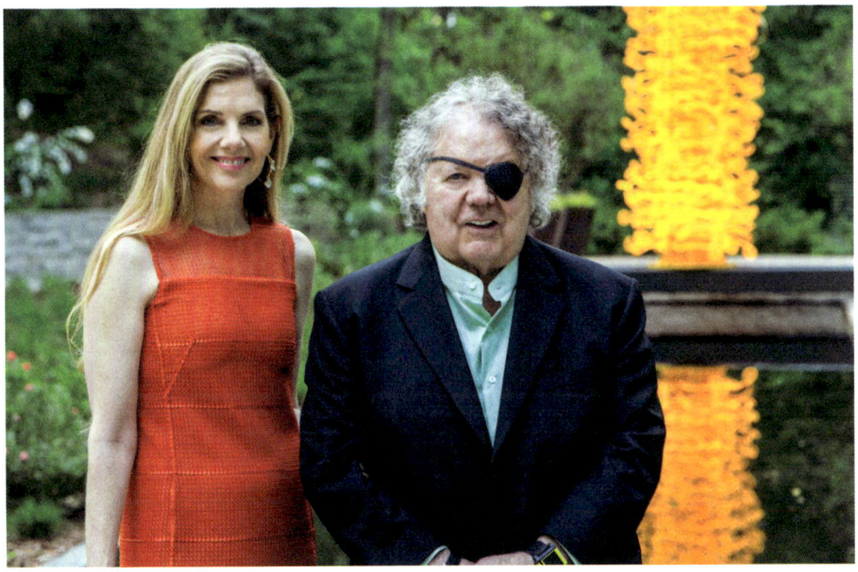

Dale and Leslie Jackson Chihuly
Atlanta Botanical Garden, 2016

Born in 1941 in Tacoma, Washington, Dale Chihuly was introduced to glass while studying interior design at the University of Washington. After graduating in 1965, Chihuly enrolled in the first glass program in the country, at the University of Wisconsin. He continued his studies at the Rhode Island School of Design (RISD), where he later established the glass program and taught for more than a decade.

In 1968, after receiving a Fulbright Fellowship, he went to work at the Venini glass factory in Venice. There he observed the team approach to blowing glass, which is critical to the way he works today. In 1971, Chihuly cofounded Pilchuck Glass School in Washington State. With this international glass center, Chihuly has led the avant-garde in the development of glass as a fine art.

His work is included in more than 200 museum collections worldwide. He has been the recipient of many awards, including twelve honorary doctorates and two fellowships from the National Endowment for the Arts.

Chihuly has created more than a dozen well-known series of works, among them, *Cylinders* and *Baskets* in the 1970s; *Seaforms*, *Macchia*, *Persians*, and *Venetians* in the 1980s; *Niijima Floats* and *Chandeliers* in the 1990s; and *Fiori* in the 2000s. He is also celebrated for large architectural installations. In 1986, he was honored with a solo exhibition, *Dale Chihuly objets de verre*, at the Musée des Arts Décoratifs, Palais du Louvre, in Paris. In 1995, he began *Chihuly Over Venice*, for which he created sculptures at glass factories in Finland, Ireland, and Mexico, then installed them over the canals and piazzas of Venice.

In 1999, Chihuly started an ambitious exhibition, *Chihuly in the Light of Jerusalem*; more than 1 million visitors attended the Tower of David Museum to view his installations. In 2001, the Victoria and Albert Museum in London curated the exhibition *Chihuly at the V&A*. Chihuly's lifelong fascination for glasshouses has grown into a series of exhibitions within botanical settings. His *Garden Cycle* began in 2001 at the Garfield Park Conservatory in Chicago. Chihuly exhibited at the Royal Botanic Gardens, Kew, near London, in 2005. Other major exhibition venues include the de Young Museum in San Francisco, in 2008; the Museum of Fine Arts, Boston, in 2011; and the Montreal Museum of Fine Arts, in 2013. *Chihuly Garden and Glass*, a long-term exhibition, opened at Seattle Center in 2012.

ATLANTA BOTANICAL GARDEN

**ART DIRECTION AND DESIGN**
Bryson Chiu, Goretti Kaomora

**EXECUTIVE CONSULTANT**
Leslie Jackson Chihuly

**COPY EDITOR**
Richard Slovak

**PHOTOGRAPHY**
Dale Chihuly, Scott M. Leen, and Terry Rishel
Image on pp. 6–7 provided by Atlanta Botanical Gardens

**COVER**
*Parterre Fountain* (detail)
2004, 54 x 92 x 95"

**FRONTISPIECE**
*Chartreuse Hornet Polyvitro Chandelier* (detail)
2001, 74 x 58 x 54"
installed 2016

**PUBLISHED BY**

CHIHULY™
WORKSHOP

P.O. Box 70856
Seattle, WA 98127
chihulyworkshop.com

ISBN 978-1-57684-059-7

Printed in Canada by Blanchette Press